9-DEZ-522

$19.95

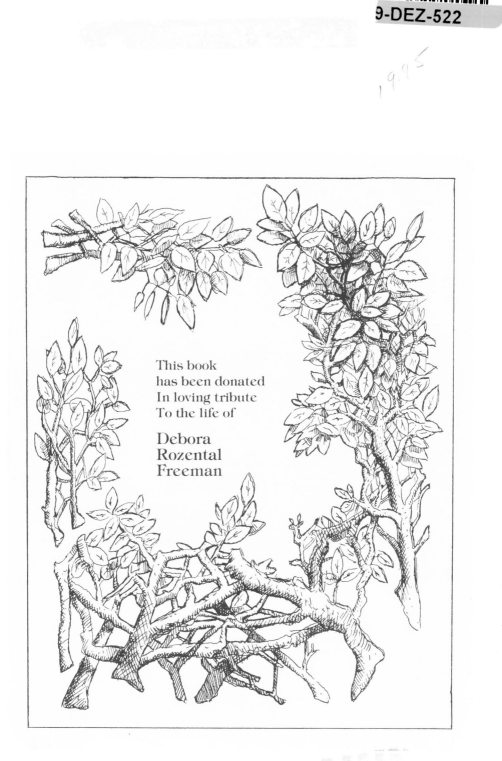

This book
has been donated
In loving tribute
To the life of

Debora
Rozental
Freeman

WITHDRAWN

Modern Critical Interpretations

George Bernard Shaw's
Major Barbara

Modern Critical Interpretations

These and other titles in preparation

Modern Critical Interpretations

George Bernard Shaw's
Major Barbara

Edited and with an introduction by

Harold Bloom
Sterling Professor of the Humanities
Yale University

Chelsea House Publishers ◊ *1988*
NEW YORK ◊ NEW HAVEN ◊ PHILADELPHIA

Highland Park Public Library

822
sh2maj
Z6

© 1988 by Chelsea House Publishers, a division
of Chelsea House Educational Communications, Inc.

Introduction © 1987 by Harold Bloom

All rights reserved. No part of this publication may be
reproduced or transmitted in any form or by any means
without the written permission of the publisher.

Printed and bound in the United States of America

10 9 8 7 6 5 4 3 2 1

∞ The paper used in this publication meets the minimum
requirements of the American National Standard for Permanence
of Paper for Printed Library Materials, Z39.48-1984.

Library of Congress Cataloging-in-Publication Data
George Bernard Shaw's Major Barbara.
   (Modern critical interpretation)
   Bibliography: p.
   Includes index.
   1. Shaw, Bernard, 1856–1950.   Major Barbara.
I. Bloom, Harold.   II. Series.
PR5363.M23G46 1988   822'.912   87–23923
ISBN 1–55546–027–5 (alk. paper)

Contents

Editor's Note

This book brings together a representative selection of what I judge to be the best modern critical interpretations of George Bernard Shaw's comedy *Major Barbara*. The critical essays are reprinted here in the chronological sequence of their original publication. I am grateful to Daniel Duffy for his aid in editing this volume.

My introduction sees *Major Barbara* as an instance of Shaw's religion of power and analyzes parallels between Shavian and Freudian visions of father-daughter relationships. Barbara Bellow Watson begins the chronological sequence of criticism by judging *Major Barbara* to be Shaw's preparatory vision of forces that could create a Platonic republic of saints, while William G. McCollom studies the limits of Shavian comic form in the play.

In Margery M. Morgan's view, *Major Barbara* implies Shaw's recognition that the true resolution of his socialist drama must take place outside the play, in society. J. L. Wisenthal applies to *Major Barbara* the Blakean dialectic of the marriage of contraries, after which Alfred Turco, Jr., judges the play to reflect a tension between Shaw's tragic view of life and the formal demands of comedy.

Comparing *Major Barbara*, as Shaw's own "problem play," to Shakespeare's *Measure for Measure*, J. Percy Smith concludes that Shaw's comedy approaches near to Euripidean tragedy. This volume ends with Stanton B. Garner, Jr.'s study of *Major Barbara* as a "comedy of disillusionment," packed with its author's intense ambivalences.

Introduction

I

"With the single exception of Homer there is no eminent writer, not even Sir Walter Scott, whom I despise so entirely as I despise Shakespear when I measure my mind against his." Shaw, obsessive polemicist, would write anything, even that unfortunate sentence. No critic would wish to measure Shaw's mind against Shakespeare's, particularly since originality was hardly Shaw's strength. Shavian ideas are quarried from Schopenhauer, Nietzsche, Ibsen, Wagner, Ruskin, Samuel Butler, Shelley, Carlyle, Marx (more or less), William Morris, Lamarck, Bergson—the list could be extended. Though an intellectual dramatist, Shaw essentially popularized the concepts and images of others. He continues to hold the stage and might appear to have earned his reputation of being the principal writer of English comic drama since Shakespeare. Yet his limitations are disconcerting, and the experience of rereading even his most famous plays, after many years away from them, is disappointingly mixed. They are much more than period pieces, but they hardly seem to be for all time. No single comedy by Shaw matches Wilde's *Importance of Being Earnest* or the tragic farces of Beckett.

Eric Bentley best demonstrated that Shaw viewed himself as a prose prophet in direct succession to Carlyle, Ruskin, and Morris. This is the Shaw of the prefaces, of *Essays in Fabian Socialism,* of *Doctors' Delusions, Crude Criminology, Sham Education.* Only the prefaces to the plays are still read, and of course they are not really prefaces to the plays. They expound Shaw's very odd personal religion, the rather cold worship of Creative Evolution. Of this religion, one can say that it is no more bizarre than most, and less distasteful than many, but it is still quite grotesque. To judge religions by aesthetic criteria may seem

1

perverse, but what others are relevant for poems, plays, stories, novels, personal essays? By any aesthetic standard, Shaw's heretical faith is considerably less interesting or impressive than D. H. Lawrence's barbaric vitalism in *The Plumed Serpent* or even Thomas Hardy's negative homage to the Immanent Will in *The Dynasts*.

G. K. Chesterton, in his book on Shaw (1909), observed that the heroine of *Major Barbara*

> ends by suggesting that she will serve God without personal hope, so that she may owe nothing to God and He owe everything to her. It does not seem to strike her that if God owes everything to her He is not God. These things affect me merely as tedious perversions of a phrase. It is as if you said, "I will never have a father unless I have begotten him."

"He who is willing to do the work gives birth to his own father," Kierkegaard wrote, and Nietzsche mused: "If one hasn't had a good father, then it is necessary to invent one." Shaw was neither a Darwinian nor a Freudian and I think he was a bad Nietzschean, who had misread rather weakly the sage of *Zarathustra*. But in his life he had suffered an inadequate father and certainly he was willing to do the work. Like his own Major Barbara, he wished to have a God who would owe everything to G. B. S. That requires a writer to possess superb mythopoeic powers, and fortunately for Shaw his greatest literary strength was as an inventor of new myths. Shaw endures in a high literary sense and remains eminently readable as well as actable because of his mythmaking faculty, a power he shared with Blake and Shelley, Wagner and Ibsen. He was not a stylist, not a thinker, not a psychologist, and utterly lacked even an iota of the uncanny Shakespearean ability to represent character and personality with overwhelming persuasiveness. His dialogue is marred by his garrulous tendencies, and the way he embodied his ideas is too often wearisomely simplistic. And yet his dramas linger in us because his beings transcend their inadequate status as representations of the human, with which he was hopelessly impatient anyway. They suggest something more obsessive than daily life, something that moves and has its being in the cosmos we learn to call Shavian, a comic version of Schopenhauer's terrible world dominated by the remorseless Will to Live.

As a critic, Shaw was genial only where he was not menaced, and he felt deeply menaced by the Aesthetic vision, of which his Socialism never quite got free. Like Oscar Wilde and Wilde's mentor Walter

Pater, Shaw was the direct descendant of Ruskin, and his animus against Wilde and Pater reflects the anxiety of an ambitious son toward rival claimants to a heritage. Pater insisted upon style, as did Wilde, and Shaw has no style to speak of, not much more, say, than Eugene O'Neill. Reviewing Wilde's *An Ideal Husband* on January 12, 1895, for Frank Harris's *Saturday Review*, Shaw was both generous and just:

> Mr. Wilde, an arch-artist, is so colossally lazy that he trifles even with the work by which an artist escapes work. He distils the very quintessence, and gets as product plays which are so unapproachably playful that they are the delight of every playgoer with twopenn'orth of brains.

A month later, confronted by *The Importance of Being Earnest: A Trivial Comedy for Serious People*, Shaw lost his composure, his generosity, and his sense of critical justice:

> I cannot say that I greatly cared for The Importance of Being Earnest. It amused me, of course; but unless comedy touches me as well as amuses me, it leaves me with a sense of having wasted my evening. I go to the theatre to be moved to laughter, not to be tickled or bustled into it; and that is why, though I laugh as much as anybody at a farcical comedy, I am out of spirits before the end of the second act, and out of temper before the end of the third, my miserable mechanical laughter intensifying these symptoms at every outburst. If the public ever becomes intelligent enough to know when it is really enjoying itself and when it is not, there will be an end of farcical comedy. Now in The Importance of Being Earnest there is plenty of this rib-tickling: for instance, the lies, the deceptions, the cross purposes, the sham mourning, the christening of the two grown-up men, the muffin eating, and so forth. These could only have been raised from the farcical plane by making them occur to characters who had, like Don Quixote, convinced us of their reality and obtained some hold on our sympathy. But that unfortunate moment of Gilbertism breaks our belief in the humanity of the play.

Would it be possible to have a sillier critical reaction to the most delightful comic drama in English since Shakespeare? Twenty-three years later, Shaw wrote a letter (if it is that) to Frank Harris, published by Harris in his *Life of Wilde* (1918), and then reprinted by Shaw in his *Pen Portraits and Reviews*. Again Wilde was an artist of "stupendous laziness," and again was indicted, this time after his death, for heartlessness:

> Our sixth meeting, the only other one I can remember, was the one at the Café Royal. On that occasion he was not too preoccupied with his danger to be disgusted with me because I, who had praised his first plays handsomely, had turned traitor over The Importance of Being Earnest. Clever as it was, it was his first really heartless play. In the others the chivalry of the eighteenth-century Irishman and the romance of the disciple of Théophile Gautier (Oscar was old-fashioned in the Irish way, except as a critic of morals) not only gave a certain kindness and gallantry to the serious passages and to the handling of the women, but provided that proximity of emotion without which laughter, however irresistible, is destructive and sinister. In The Importance of Being Earnest this had vanished; and the play, though extremely funny, was essentially hateful. I had no idea that Oscar was going to the dogs, and that this represented a real degeneracy produced by his debaucheries. I thought he was still developing; and I hazarded the unhappy guess that The Importance of Being Earnest was in idea a young work written or projected long before under the influence of Gilbert and furbished up for Alexander as a potboiler. At the Café Royal that day I calmly asked him whether I was not right. He indignantly repudiated my guess, and said loftily (the only time he ever tried on me the attitude he took to John Gray and his more abject disciples) that he was disappointed in me. I suppose I said, "Then what on earth has happened to you?" but I recollect nothing more on that subject except that we did not quarrel over it.

Shaw remains unique in finding *The Importance of Being Earnest* (of all plays!) "essentially hateful." A clue to this astonishing reaction can be found in Shaw's outraged response to Max Beerbohm's review of *Man and Superman*, as expressed in his letter to Beerbohm, on September 15, 1903:

> You idiot, do you suppose I dont know my own powers? I tell you in this book as plainly as the thing can be told, that

the reason Bunyan reached such a pitch of mastery in literary art (and knew it) whilst poor Pater could never get beyond a nerveless amateur affectation which had not even the common workaday quality of vulgar journalism (and, alas! didnt know it, though he died of his own futility), was that it was life or death with the tinker to make people understand his message and see his vision, whilst Pater had neither message nor vision & only wanted to cultivate style, with the result that of the two attempts I have made to read him the first broke down at the tenth sentence & the second at the first. Pater took a genteel walk up Parnassus: Bunyan fled from the wrath to come: that explains the difference in their pace & in the length they covered.

Poor Pater is dragged in and beaten up because he was the apostle of style, while Bunyan is summoned up supposedly as the model for Shaw, who also has a message and a vision. It is a little difficult to associate *The Pilgrim's Progress* with *Man and Superman*, but one can suspect shrewdly that Pater here is a surrogate for Wilde, who had achieved an absolute comic music of perfect style and stance in *The Importance of Being Earnest*. Shavians become indignant at the comparison, but Shaw does poorly when one reads side by side any of the *Fabian Essays* and Wilde's extraordinary essay "The Soul of Man under Socialism." Something even darker happens when we juxtapose *Man and Superman* with *The Importance of Being Earnest*, but then Shaw is not unique in not being able to survive such a comparison.

II

Shaw initially planned to call *Major Barbara* by the rather more imposing title of *Andrew Undershaft's Profession*. The play has been so popular (deservedly so) that we cannot think of it by any other title, but the earlier notion would have emphasized Undershaft's strength and centrality. He dwarfs Cusins, and dominates Barbara, as much during her rebellion against him as in her return. And he raises the fascinating question of Shaw's own ambivalence toward the Socialist ideal, despite Shaw's lifelong labor in behalf of that ideal. Undershaft may be the archetype of the capitalist as amoral munitions-monger, but his arms establishment dangerously resembles a benign state socialism, and the drama moves finally in a direction equally available for interpretation by the extreme Left or the extreme Right.

Despite his ignorance of Freud, Shaw in *Major Barbara* (1905) wrote a drama wholly consonant with Freud's contemporary works, *The Interpretation of Dreams* and *Three Essays on the Theory of Sexuality*. Consider the first amiable confrontation of Barbara and her father Undershaft, who has not seen her since she was a baby:

> UNDERSHAFT: For me there is only one true morality; but it might not fit you, as you do not manufacture aerial battleships. There is only one true morality for every man; but every man has not the same true morality.
>
> LOMAX [*overtaxed*]: Would you mind saying that again? I didnt quite follow it.
>
> CUSINS: It's quite simple. As Euripides says, one man's meat is another man's poison morally as well as physically.
>
> UNDERSHAFT: Precisely.
>
> LOMAX: Oh, that! Yes, yes, yes. True. True.
>
> STEPHEN: In other words, some men are honest and some are scoundrels.
>
> BARBARA: Bosh! There are no scoundrels.
>
> UNDERSHAFT: Indeed? Are there any good men?
>
> BARBARA: No. Not one. There are neither good men nor scoundrels: there are just children of one Father; and the sooner they stop calling one another names the better. You neednt talk to me: I know them. Ive had scores of them through my hands: scoundrels, criminals, infidels, philanthropists, missionaries, county councillors, all sorts. Theyre all just the same sort of sinner; and theres the same salvation ready for them all.
>
> UNDERSHAFT: May I ask have you ever saved a maker of cannons?
>
> BARBARA: No. Will you let me try?
>
> UNDERSHAFT: Well, I will make a bargain with you. If I go to see you tomorrow in your Salvation Shelter, will you come the day after to see me in my cannon works?
>
> BARBARA: Take care. It may end in your giving up the cannons for the sake of the Salvation Army.
>
> UNDERSHAFT: Are you sure it will not end in your giving up the Salvation Army for the sake of the cannons?

BARBARA: I will take my chance of that.

UNDERSHAFT: And I will take my chance of the other. [*They shake hands on it.*] Where is your shelter?

BARBARA: In West Ham. At the sign of the cross. Ask anybody in Canning Town. Where are your works?

UNDERSHAFT: In Perivale St Andrews. At the sign of the sword. Ask anybody in Europe.

LOMAX: Hadnt I better play something?

BARBARA: Yes. Give us Onward, Christian Soldiers.

LOMAX: Well, thats rather a strong order to begin with, dont you know. Suppose I sing Thourt passing hence, my brother. It's much the same tune.

BARBARA: It's too melancholy. You get saved, Cholly; and youll pass hence, my brother, without making such a fuss about it.

LADY BRITOMART: Really, Barbara, you go on as if religion were a pleasant subject. Do have some sense of propriety.

UNDERSHAFT: I do not find it an unpleasant subject, my dear. It is the only one that capable people really care for.

Barbara, having replaced the absent Undershaft by God the Father in his Salvation Army guise, begins by accepting her phallic father as one more sinner to be saved. Their prophetic interchange of signs—daughterly cross and fatherly sword—bonds them against the mother, as each stands for a version of the only subject that the capable Shaw really cares for: religion as the Life Force, Creative Evolution. The daughter and the father, in mutual recognition, have commenced upon their inevitably narcissistic dance of repressed psychosexual courtship. Cusins shrewdly sums up the enigma in his act 2 dialogue with Undershaft:

UNDERSHAFT: Religion is our business at present, because it is through religion alone that we can win Barbara.

CUSINS: Have you, too, fallen in love with Barbara?

UNDERSHAFT: Yes, with a father's love.

CUSINS: A father's love for a grown-up daughter is the most dangerous of all infatuations. I apologize for mentioning my own pale, coy, mistrustful fancy in the same breath with it.

Undershaft's love for Barbara is conversionary and therefore complex; its aim is to transform family romance into societal romance.

After three quarters of a century, G. K. Chesterton remains much the best of Shaw's early critics, but he insisted upon a weak misreading of Undershaft's (and Shaw's) scheme:

> The ultimate epigram of *Major Barbara* can be put thus. People say that poverty is no crime; Shaw says that poverty is a crime; that it is a crime to endure it, a crime to be content with it, that it is the mother of all crimes of brutality, corruption, and fear. If a man says to Shaw that he is born of poor but honest parents, Shaw tells him that the very word "but" shows that his parents were probably dishonest. In short, he maintains here what he had maintained elsewhere: that what the people at this moment require is not more patriotism or more art or more religion or more morality or more sociology, but simply more money. The evil is not ignorance or decadence or sin or pessimism; the evil is poverty. The point of this particular drama is that even the noblest enthusiasm of the girl who becomes a Salvation Army officer fails under the brute money power of her father who is a modern capitalist. When I have said this it will be clear why this play, fine and full of bitter sincerity as it is, must in a manner be cleared out of the way before we come to talk of Shaw's final and serious faith. For this serious faith is in the sanctity of human will, in the divine capacity for creation and choice rising higher than environment and doom; and so far as that goes, *Major Barbara* is not only apart from his faith but against his faith. *Major Barbara* is an account of environment victorious over heroic will. There are a thousand answers to the ethic in *Major Barbara* which I should be inclined to offer. I might point out that the rich do not so much buy honesty as curtains to cover dishonesty: that they do not so much buy health as cushions to comfort disease. And I might suggest that the doctrine that poverty degrades the poor is much more likely to be used as an argument for keeping them powerless than as an argument for making them rich. But there is no need to find such answers to the materialistic pessimism of *Major Barbara*. The best answer to it is in Shaw's own best and crowning philosophy.

Is the environment of Undershaft's "spotlessly clean and beautiful hillside town" of well-cared-for munitions workers victorious over

Barbara's heroic will? Has the sanctity of human will, its divine capacity for creation and choice, been violated by Undershaft playing the part of Machiavel? Who could be more Shavian than the great Life Forcer, Undershaft, who cheerfully provides the explosives with which the present can blast itself into the future, in a perhaps involuntary parody of Creative Evolution? How far is Undershaft from the Caesar of *Caesar and Cleopatra*? The questions are so self-answering as to put Chesterton, splendid as he is, out of court.

But that still gives us the problem of Barbara's conversion: to what precisely has she come? The scene of her instruction is a characteristic Shavian outrage, persuasive and absurd. Cusins asks Undershaft the crucial question as to his munitions enterprise: "What drives the place?"

> UNDERSHAFT [*enigmatically*]: A will of which I am a part.
>
> BARBARA [*startled*]: Father! Do you know what you are saying; or are you laying a snare for my soul?
>
> CUSINS: Dont listen to his metaphysics, Barbara. The place is driven by the most rascally part of society, the money hunters, the pleasure hunters, the military promotion hunters; and he is their slave.
>
> UNDERSHAFT: Not necessarily. Remember the Armorer's Faith. I will take an order from a good man as cheerfully as from a bad one. If you good people prefer preaching and shirking to buying my weapons and fighting the rascals, dont blame me. I can make cannons: I cannot make courage and conviction. Bah! you tire me, Euripides, with your morality mongering. Ask Barbara: she understands. [*He suddenly reaches up and takes Barbara's hands, looking powerfully into her eyes.*] Tell him, my love, what power really means.
>
> BARBARA [*hypnotized*]: Before I joined the Salvation Army, I was in my own power; and the consequence was that I never knew what to do with myself. When I joined it, I had not time enough for all the things I had to do.
>
> UNDERSHAFT [*approvingly*]: Just so. And why was that, do you suppose?
>
> BARBARA: Yesterday I should have said, because I was in the power of God. [*She resumes her self-possession, withdrawing her hands from his with a power equal to his own.*] But

you came and shewed me that I was in the power of Bodger and Undershaft. Today I feel—oh! how can I put it into words? Sarah: do you remember the earthquake at Cannes, when we were little children?—how little the surprise of the first shock mattered compared to the dread and horror of waiting for the second? That is how I feel in this place today. I stood on the rock I thought eternal; and without a word of warning it reeled and crumbled under me. I was safe with an infinite wisdom watching me, an army marching to Salvation with me; and in a moment, at a stroke of your pen in a cheque book, I stood alone; and the heavens were empty. That was the first shock of the earthquake: I am waiting for the second.

There will not be a second shock, nor need there be. The dialectic of Barbara's conversion is all there in the single moment when Undershaft speaks of "a will of which I am a part" and Barbara is startled into the realization that her two fathers, Undershaft and God, are one. The realization is confirmed in the covenant of power that springs up between father and daughter as Undershaft takes Barbara's hands, while hypnotizing her through the will of which he is a part. Having been driven by one version of the Life Force, she yields now to another, but it is the same force. We somehow wish to find Shavian irony here, but there is less than we seek to find. What we discover is Shavian cruelty at Barbara's expense. Yielding her will to Undershaft sends Barbara into a massive regression, which calls into question her Christian idealism at the play's opening. A baby clutching at her mother's skirt, poor Barbara ends as the most reduced and humiliated heroine anywhere in Shaw. Why is he so harsh to so vivacious a figure, exuberant in her early idealism?

Eric Bentley observes accurately that "Barbara's final conversion has much less force than her previous disillusionment." This is useful as far as it goes, but Bentley is too fond of Shaw to see and say that her final conversion destroys her as an adult. *Major Barbara* is not a text for feminists, and if it can be construed as one for socialists, then they are very unsocial socialists indeed. Undershaft was a brilliant indication of where Shaw was heading, toward Carlyle's worship of heroes, strong men who would impose socialism because the Superman still waited to be born. Playful, wise, and charming, Undershaft nevertheless is a dangerous vision of the father-god enforcing the will of Creative Evolution. One remembers that Shaw, though knowing better, always retained a fondness for Stalin.

Nothing is got for nothing, and Shaw makes Barbara pay the price for this extravagant triumph of the religion of power. To be reconciled with the father, she becomes a child again, in a very curious parody of the Christian second birth. Perhaps she is a Shavian self-punishment that masquerades as a Nietzschean will revenging itself against time. Her pathetic dwindling remains a dark tonality at the conclusion of one of Shaw's most enduring farces.

Sainthood for Millionaires

Barbara Bellow Watson

The major difficulty of *Major Barbara* lies in its simple and necessary
irony, which is only the irony of life itself. Shaw, in his preface to the
play, gives copious "First Aid to Critics," but the confusion remains,
partly because, as he himself points out, if you tell the truth nobody
will believe you, and partly because this preface deals with ideas rather
than with dramatic method. That method is, as Chesterton calls it,
"the grave, solemn and sacred joke for which the play itself was
written," an irony designed to show that we may not accept the least
of capitalism's benefits without acceping the last of its depredations:
also that the damage it does and the audacity of its excuses beggar
invective and so thoroughly satirize themselves that no response is left
but irony, a weapon Shaw wields as superbly as Swift. There is even a
modest echo of *A Modest Proposal* in the preface:

> Suppose we were to abolish all penalties for such activities as
> burglary, arson, rape and murder, and decide that poverty is
> the one thing we will not tolerate—that every adult with less
> than, say, £365 a year, shall be painlessly but inexorably
> killed, and every hungry half naked child forcibly fattened
> and clothed, would not that be an enormous improvement
> on our existing system, which has already destroyed so
> many civilizations, and is visibly destroying ours in the
> same way?

From *Modern Drama* 11, no. 3 (December 1968). © 1968 by A. C. Edwards.

But the philosophy of the play is far from being a "materialistic pessimism" as Chesterton claims. Chesterton, a Christian, was poignantly aware that Barbara's belief in her work for the Salvation Army comes down in ruins, although the nobility and the sincerity of that belief remain standing. Money and power rise triumphant. But, as the play shows once its irony is understood, neither the Christian thesis nor the capitalist anti-thesis carries the ultimate day. That belongs to the third religion in the play, Shaw's secular religion of Creative Evolution, which is closely related to his socialism. It is the Life Force that wants the marriage of Cusins and Barbara. It is also the Life Force that has led Undershaft to adopt his religion and his success—one and the same—for in the vital genius the Life Force runs powerfully towards its objects—and attracts others irresistibly.

The central conflict of the play is between the ideas of Andrew Undershaft on the one hand, and the ideas of the whole society, represented by his whole family, on the other. St. Andrew (canonized in Shaw's preface, not in the play) lives by money and gunpowder; nothing remarkable in that, except that he is not ashamed to admit it. Opposed to him stand his daughter, a major in the Salvation Army, who believes intensely in the Christian virtues and not at all in money; his estranged wife, Lady Britomart, an aristocrat with no nonsense about her; his lesser children, Stephen, a worldly weakling, and Sarah, a nonentity; and Barbara's fiancé, a professor of Greek and something of a poet. Given the fact that Barbara, the central force in this opposition, is a realist like her father, in spite of being a missionary, the outcome of the drama is inevitable. Undershaft has (sometimes silently) the last word in every argument. And he has something better than the last word: he had the last act. He has, in other words, not only convincing arguments, which would always be countered by other convincing arguments (Chesterton offers a few, cogent in themselves, but dramatically false), but also the reversal of all the stubbornly held opinions of his opponents. In a clean sweep of the board, Undershaft converts to his own view the representatives of Christian spirituality, of academic classicism, of the old aristocracy, and even the limp indifference of the idle rich. All are forced to recognize the unity of body and soul, the fusion of money with morality. In the model town that so persuades them, the aristocrat sees power and order, the professor of Greek sees lucidity, and the Salvation Army lass sees liberation of the spirit. Not that this conversion is made easy for them. Undershaft displays no redeeming sentimentalities, but insists on all his infamies, following the logic of the capitalist structure to its last iron law, its last starving innocent, its last bath of blood and fire.

Now all this is paradoxical only if we expect a socialist author to render simplistic fantasies in which virtue (poverty) triumphs over vice (money and power), or suffers in the right way, without exercising the intellect at all. Although it is perfectly true that all his plays are polemical in the strictest sense, the essential difference between Shaw and the ordinary writer of didactic plays is that the message is not mouthed by the actors or moralized by artificial rewards and punishments, but embodied in the living movement of the drama. Hence the theme of *Major Barbara* is not by any means the beneficence of capitalism (the products of capitalism being miserably on display in act 2), not even the necessity of cannons. Instead the theme is an ironic egg within a visible shell. The shell, an inclusive idea that pervades Shaw's work early and late, is the necessity of realism. Here a distinction must be drawn. The supposed realism of those who accept the *status quo* out of indifference abetted by stupidity, like Sarah and Charles, or out of moral cowardice of the intellect, like Mrs. Baines, is at the opposite pole from the genuine realism of the Undershaft mind that accepts no catchwords and pretends no unfelt feelings. Cynical realists like Charles Lomax, are in truth of the Devil's party without knowing it. Chesterton says:

> The truth is that the ordinary anti-humanitarian only manages to harden his heart by having already softened his head. It is the reverse of sentimental to insist that a colonial is being burned alive; for sentimentalism must be the clinging to pleasant thoughts. And no one, not even a Higher Evolutionist, can think a colonial burned alive a pleasant thought. The sentimental thing is to warm your hands at the fire while denying the existence of the colonial, and that is the ruling habit in England, as it has been the chief business of Bernard Shaw to show. And in this the brutalitarians hate him not because he is soft, but because he is hard, because he is not softened by conventional excuses; because he looks hard at a thing—and hits harder.

This liberation from cant leads quite inevitably to Major Barbara's discovery of the yolk in the ironic egg: the idea that capitalism as a system is so pervasive and so corrupting that it makes even charity into an evil force. The Salvation Army prevents riots, fends off revolution:

> CUSINS: I dont think you quite know what the Army does for the poor.
>
> UNDERSHAFT: Oh yes I do. It draws their teeth: that is enough for me as a man of business.
>
> CUSINS: Nonsense! It makes them sober—
>
> UNDERSHAFT: I prefer sober workmen. The profits are larger.
>
> CUSINS: —honest—
>
> UNDERSHAFT: Honest workmen are the most economical.
>
> CUSINS: —attached to their homes—
>
> UNDERSHAFT: So much the better: they will put up anything rather than change their shop.
>
> CUSINS: —happy—
>
> UNDERSHAFT: An invaluable safeguard against revolution.
>
> CUSINS: —unselfish—
>
> UNDERSHAFT: Indifferent to their own interest, which suits me exactly.
>
> CUSINS: —with their thoughts on heavenly things—
>
> UNDERSHAFT: And not on Trade Unionism nor Socialism. Excellent.
>
> CUSINS: You really are an infernal old rascal.

Furthermore, this Army feeds and shelters the body in return for dishonesty of the spirit, a rotten bargain wherever it is made. Mrs. Baines is as blind to this, and Barbara early in the play as naive, as the missionaries in *A Passage to India:*

> Old Mr. Graysford and young Mr. Sorley made converts during a famine, because they distributed food; but when times improved they were naturally left alone again, and though surprised and aggrieved each time this happened, they never learnt wisdom.

It is a mockery to attempt religion in a soul whose body is sore beset by the seven deadly sins: "Food, clothing, firing, rent, taxes, respectability and children." But religion is not a mockery at Perivale St. Andrews, where Undershaft has, as a moment's thought will show, set up a little island of private enterprise socialism, an exemplar of all that socialism might be. In this earthly paradise, created by a man who is labelled throughout the play with tags that suggest the devil, capitalism has been only a means to an end. In the last scene there is even an indication that the guns may be also a means to the same utopian end. This is hardly a plea for capitalism.

And behind the polemical structure of the play stands the polemical explanation of the preface. But Shaw's "First Aid to Critics" does less to explain his attitude toward Undershaft than certain remarks in the preface to *Mrs Warren's Profession*. In both cases a vital character has to choose between poverty (practical) and "infamy" (spiritual) and both are extreme cases chosen to strip the principle mercilessly. Both Undershaft and Mrs. Warren choose prostitution. The whole mystery of *Major Barbara* vanishes when we see Undershaft's dilemma in Mrs. Warren's:

> Though it is quite natural and *right* for Mrs. Warren to choose what is, according to her lights, the least immoral alternative, it is none the less infamous of society to offer such alternatives. For the alternatives offered are not morality and immorality, but two sorts of immorality.

Seen in these terms, the choice between honest poverty and unscrupulous riches is an outmoded melodramatic cliché completely superseded by the choice between an immoral society and a moral society. The significance of millionaries changes radically. Balanced by Peter Shirley, his counterpart at the other end of the economic scale, our millionaire is an eloquent hyperbole, another example of that figure of speech so dear to Shaw's prose and so pitifully inadequate to the expression of our wars, our cruelties, our hypocrisies. This millionaire is, in other words, an attempt to open desperate darkness by a desperate illumination. For only the greatest munitions maker in England can, by a calm insistence on the Undershaft motto, "Unashamed," convey the shame that attaches to every one of us for our complicity in the crimes of capitalism. "The notion that you can earmark certain coins as tainted is an unpractical individualist superstition." This much Shaw had already established in *Widowers' Houses* and *Mrs Warren's Profession*. In *Major Barbara*, he goes further, putting a more insistent pressure on the limits of our complacency, and going one step beyond the guilt to the responsibility. The

> enthusiastic young clergyman of the Established Church . . . cannot help himself by refusing to accept money from anybody except sweet old ladies with independent incomes and gentle and lovely ways of life. He has only to follow up the income of the sweet ladies to its industrial source, and there he will find Mrs. Warren's profession and the poisonous canned meat and all the rest of it. His own stipend has the same root. He must either share the world's guilt or go

to another planet. He must save the world's honor if he is
to save his own.

Undershaft does just this. He at least is without self-deception. And he
has also taken a step in the direction of saving the world's honor. As
poor-but-honest teachers, mothers, writers, professional reformers and
such, we are all too quick to excuse complicity by ranking its degrees,
or to mask it under some disguise that conceals guilt but cures nothing. Speaking of an assassination attempt in Madrid, Shaw reminds us
of a truth that applies equally well to terrorism of any kind:

> he launches his sixpennorth of fulminate, missing his mark,
> but scattering the bowels of as many horses as any bull in
> the arena, and slaying twentythree persons, besides wound-
> ing ninetynine. And of all these, the horses alone are inno-
> cent of the guilt he is avenging: had he blown all Madrid to
> atoms with every adult person in it, not one could have
> escaped the charge of being an accessory, before, at, and
> after the fact, to poverty and prostitution, to such wholesale
> massacre of infants as Herod never dreamt of, to plague,
> pestilence and famine, battle, murder and lingering death—
> perhaps not one who had not helped, through example,
> precept, connivance, and even clamor, to teach the dyna-
> miter his well-learnt gospel of hatred and vengeance, by
> approving every day of sentences of years of imprisonment
> so infernal in their unnatural stupitity and panic-stricken
> cruelty, that their advocates can disavow neither the dagger
> nor the bomb without stripping the mask of justice and
> humanity from themselves also.

Besides denying us the moral superiority to millionaires that we
all clutch to our Pharisaic bosoms, Undershaft serves a second purpose. He is a reminder that, in any such world as ours, even as an
individual, the man who accepts poverty is a social liability, both an
active and a passive force for evil. Here is Shaw speaking *ex cathedra:*

> Now what does this Let Him Be Poor mean? It means let
> him be weak. Let him be ignorant. Let him become a
> nucleus of disease. Let him be a standing exhibition and
> example of ugliness and dirt. Let him have rickety children.
> Let him be cheap, and drag his fellows down to his own
> price by selling himself to do their work. Let his habitations

turn our cities into poisonous congeries of slums. Let his daughters infect our young men with the diseases of the streets, and his sons revenge him by turning the nation's manhood into scrofula, cowardice, cruelty, hypocrisy, political imbecility, and all the other fruits of oppression and malnutrition. Let the undeserving become still less deserving; and let the deserving lay up for himself, not treasures in heaven, but horrors in hell upon earth. This being so, is it really wise to let him be poor? Would he not do ten times less harm as a prosperous burglar, incendiary, ravisher or murderer, to the utmost limits of humanity's comparatively negligible impulses in these directions?

A hundred learned commissions have sat since those words were written and have told us no more about the active dangers of poverty.

As to the passive dangers, in the Shavian theater early and late, the vital genius refuses martyrdom of this kind. All very well for Dick Dudgeon in *The Devil's Disciple* to put his neck into the noose out of a sense of honor (*l'acte gratuit* in an unfamiliar flavor), but the martyrdom of poverty produces the opposite result, loss of self-respect (not to mention teeth and other desirable attributes), and is rejected by Mrs. Warren, who knows what the white lead factory does to a woman, by Violet, in *Man and Superman*, who knows that a husband with no money is no use as a husband, by Eliza Doolittle, who labors up out of the gutter in *Pygmalion*, by Ellie Dunn, daughter of an idealist, who is ready to sell herself to a repulsive millionaire in *Heartbreak House* because a soul is more expensive than a body, and most spectacularly in *The Millionairess*, by a lady who outdoes Undershaft in ruthlessness, which she loves for its own sake as few love milder virtues.

And Shaw reminds us again and again that any man or woman who sees how capitalism works, must either replace it or use it for his own survival. He is not one of those who believe that individual acts of anarchistic protest will gradually inspire some incalculable degree of rebellion in "the people" and lead to the revolution that will sweep all this away. And surely the increasing political conservatism of the labor unions in the last quarter century indicates that the working class is more inclined to reason like Andrew Undershaft than to reason like Karl Marx. But Shaw does more than justify the munitions millionaire as a private person. (One thundering denunciation in the Shavian vocabulary is powerfully cadenced up to the phrase, "a hopelessly

Private Person.") The insistent lesson of the play is that Undershaft (as even that chief of denigrators, the ex-wife, must finally admit) is socially as well as personally sound. The demonstration is logical to a wonder, but only if we take note of the missing term supplied in the second act. In act 1 the major and the millionaire assert their opposed values: the soul and the pound sterling, or the Christian-social and the pagan-selfish points of view. In act 3 these resolve into a harmony so large that it sweeps into it the intellect of the ivory tower—Cusins—and the energy of the old aristocracy—Lady Britomart—in a joyful inclusiveness like the finale of Beethoven's Ninth, but returned at the last moment to a poignantly small comic diapason that reminds us we still live in this world as men have made it. The great sound, of which I have more to say later, the synthesis that does not yet exist in this world, is off-stage, but it controls the ulimate meaning of the play. And only the vital genius, the man who has both brains and fight, and puts them to use on the side of life, can move society. But it is quite significant that in the Shavian theater the vital genius is so often a woman, which brings us back from Undershaft to his daughter.

Most certainly Barbara is her father's daughter. *Major Barbara* is also a family drama, as social as it is socialist. In fact, the public and private questions are no less interwoven than in *Oedipus Rex* or *Hamlet*. Besides her father, the heroine has a strong mother, a brother and sister, both nonentities, a prospective brother-in-law more null than all the rest, and a remarkable fiancé of her own. Among all these, Shaw schematizes and dramatizes the interplay of moral forces in society. In fact, since Undershaft's money and munitions are the real power behind the government of England, the drama may be said to expand to the same heroic magnitude as Greek or Elizabethan tragedy, but transposed into a key so different that we fail to recognize the old theme.

The strong bond between father and daughter is treated early and late in his career by Shaw, who did not wait for Freud to point it out to him. This theme interests him far more than mother-son relationships, largely because the mother's influence on the son seems to transmit weakness, while the fathers in question are usually unconventional and strong-willed men who (quite plausibly, as ordinary fathers will not think of training a *daughter* up to be a great man) consciously create strength and independence in their daughters. The necessary condition is, of course, that these fathers leave enough money to support an independent spirit, otherwise an intolerable luxury for a woman, since Shaw never fails to take into account that fact that female slavery (inside marriage or out) is firmly based on economic dependence and not, as presumably in the Stone Age, on biological factors. In *Cashel Byron's Profession*, his novel of 1886, the heroine horrifies all her Victorian acquaintances by talking unconventional common sense taught to her by her father, and by falling in love with an athlete for the sake of his physical beauty. In *The Millionairess* (1936), another daughter in love with the memory of a strong father triumphs over convention in every conceivable department. In *Major Barbara*, father and daughter interest each other at once when they meet as adults. This relationship is subtler and more dramatic. Since the Undershaft children do not know their father and have been brought up to deplore him (rather like the Clandon-Crampton clan, children of another strong mother and discarded father, in *You Never Can Tell*), there is both recognition and reversal in the return of Barbara from the blood-and-fire banner of her father in heaven to the blood and fire business of her father on earth. These two recognize each other at the end of act 1 by an affinity of spirit more unmistakable than the strawberry marks in the old stories. Cusins acknowledges the bond when he says teasingly:

> A father's love for a grown-up daughter is the most danger-
> ous of all infatuations. I apologize for mentioning my own
> pale, coy, mistrustful fancy in the same breath with it.

And the Grecian overtones of mysterious intervention of fate (conso-nant with the subject Cusins professes) are strengthened indirectly when the long-lost daughter is found to have provided her foundling father with the very foundling son-in-law he needs. The Undershaft tradition requires that the business be handed down to an adopted son, and Barbara has unconsciously provided this quasi-incestuous heir. For the square knot of this family's relationship is tied even tighter when the reconciliation of father and daughter draws with it his former wife and her future husband into a community of sympathetic equals.

The schematic relation of Barbara with her mother is quite differ-ent. While the father functions psychologically and symbolically, the mother, Lady Britomart, is most interesting seen historically. She is unique among Shavian mothers, who, when they appear at all in Shaw's drama, neglect, pet and bully their sons, hamper and mislead their daughters. Some, like Mrs. Whitefield in *Man and Superman* and

Mrs. Collins in *Getting Married* are so thoroughly subjugated by Victorian womanism that they are merely ineffectual, bewildered burdens on their competent children. The genuine crabby tyrant of the puritan fireside, like Mrs. Dudgeon in *The Devil's Disciple*, appears very seldom. But caricatures are not needed. Even the most enlightened mother, Mrs. Clandon in *You Never Can Tell*, is quite impossible. She is an Advanced Woman, theory-ridden and self-conscious in the extreme, and she fails precisely because of her determination to succeed, to form her children into models of future humanity. She and Lady Britomart make the same mistakes, in both theory and practice, by assuming that life can be ladylike, and by cutting their children off from an imperfect father.

But Lady Britomart contains woman's unrealized potential, which shows itself best (as Shaw makes clear in *Misalliance*) in the aristocracy, whose women are neither hobbled by middle-class respectability nor crushed by the weight of poverty. True, this overpowering dowager is a stock figure of comedy, and Lady Britomart is introduced at the beginning of act 1 in just this way. Superficially, she is like Lady Bracknell in Wilde's *The Importance of Being Earnest*, a woman whose husband must either abjectly submit, like Lord Bracknell, or leave home, like Undershaft. Nevertheless, the opening scene shows her son as a natural object for bullying. And, unlike Lady Bracknell, a pure comic figure, Lady Britomart moves her whole monolithic presence into the new world, and in moving shows us how much more she potentially is than the elegant bully of comedy. For though Wilde's dowager (and her daughter) are portrayed with all the accuracy of caricature, they are frozen in their entrancing poses, but Lady Britomart, her daughter, and all Shavian heroines are able to move and breathe, simply because Shaw likes women and understands what makes them tick, viz:

> I am a dramatic author, and people wonder what is the secret of my extraordinary knowledge of women which enchants the whole world. Women come to me and ask: "Where did you get this amazing knowledge of women?" Very often I am suspected of having in the course of my life been a most abandoned character, and that is how I acquired this knowledge. But I never acquired it at all. I always assumed that a woman was a person exactly like myself, and that is how the trick is done.

The comment applies most fully to the fully realized character of Major Barbara, but behind her stands Lady Britomart, who contains in herself the qualities that, in the next generation, emancipated from the fierce corsetry of Victorian rules, must resolve themselves either into the freedom and energy of her daughter Barbara or into the nullity of Sarah. The difference between the two daughters is reinforced by the difference between their fiancés. The imbecilic Lomax "likes Sarah and thinks it will be rather a lark to marry her." Cusins, the character derived from Gilbert Murray, Regius Professor of Greek at Oxford during the early part of this century, is a man of intellect, poise and passion, whose state of mind is accurately characterized by Lady Britomart when she says he "went to the Salvation Army to worship Barbara and nothing else." The word "worship" combines colloquialism with the religious overtone that Shaw intends. For not two but three religions are present in this play: the Salvation Army's, Undershaft's, and Shaw's—Creative Evolution. It is the last of these that triumphs, even though it is not understood, scarcely mentioned, by any character in the play. It is the Life Force that leads many a Shavian hero into the arms of a vital genius, although he should—and does—know better. On the other hand, the Life Force does not depend on mystical apprehensions. Like all the attractive women in Shaw's works, Barbara Undershaft has the energy that is the eternal delight of Shavian suitors. And Cusins, like other Shavian heroes, makes the not entirely foolish assumption that a girl who is good at one sort of thing will be good at another. He puts the classic Shavian case with the calm of a desperate lucidity when he says:

> Mr. Undershaft: I am in many ways a weak, timid, ineffectual person; and my health is far from satisfactory. But whenever I feel that I must have anything, I get it, sooner or later. I feel that way about Barbara. I dont like marriage; I feel intensely afraid of it; and I dont know what I shall do with Barbara or what she will do with me. But I feel that I and nobody else must marry her. Please regard that as settled.—Not that I wish to be arbitrary; but why should I waste your time discussing what is inevitable?

Or, as Shaw puts it in his stage direction for Cusins's entrance: "By the operation of some instinct which is not merciful enough to blind him with the illusions of love, he is obstinately bent on marrying

Barbara." His enslavement goes further than this. In act 2 Cusins makes a confession:

> Yes, a confession. Listen, all. Until I met Barbara I thought myself in the main an honorable, truthful man, because I wanted the approval of my conscience more than I wanted anything else. But the moment I saw Barbara, I wanted her far more than the approval of my conscience.

And here again Shaw insists on the extreme case in order to sharpen the edge of his argument. Such abjectness is normally portrayed only as an example of the horrible dominance of the female, which leads some men to say things like:

> You may add that in the hive and the anthill we see fully realized the two things that some of us must dread for our own species—the dominance of the female and the dominance of the collective.

But Shaw, as I have already pointed out, sees women as people like himself, a compliment we should be quick to accept. And in the dramatic working-out of this relationship it is quite clear that Cusins, though he may think himself enslaved to a woman, is in fact enslaved to the Life Force that makes itself felt through her, no less in her social crusading than in her sexual charm. Tanner, in *Man and Superman*, is pursued and entrapped by Ann Whitefield, and, as one realist comments: "I dunno about the bee and the spider. But the marked down victim, that's what you are and no mistake; and a jolly good job for you, too, I should say." We are not allowed to doubt for one moment that Tanner's resistance and capitulation are anything but a delightful dance of the mating season. Even more so in the case of Cusins, whose beloved has other things on her mind than husband-hunting. The effect would be quite different if Barbara were really her mother all over again. It is amusing enough that one of Oscar Wilde's young men should remark: "All women become like their mothers; that is their tragedy. No man does; that is his." But the truth, as Wilde points out elsewhere, is never pure and very seldom simple. Between mother and daughter, in this case, two factors intervene to create a considerable change. First, the difference of a generation puts Barbara into the period of the liberated woman, though she is an early example. Second, she is a vital genius, one of a long line of such women in Shaw's plays, and of them all Barbara is most like Saint Joan, a character who needs none of the hampering protection of Wilton Circle or the circling camouflage of petticoats. Both heroines work in uniform—or, to be exact, out of the normal uniform for women. In the same way, their relations with men are outside all ordinary patterns. Saint Joan is not the camp follower conventional gossips assume her to be. Neither does Barbara fit the expected patterns in her dealings with Cusins. In fact, she reverses even the established Shavian pattern, the pursuit of the man by the woman, for her magnetism is so powerful that Cusins, a man of unusual personal dignity, literally joins the parade that follows after her. This is not bullying, unless we accuse the cosmos of bullying. The test of the relationship comes at the moment when Cusins must make his final choice, knowing that if he chooses wrong he may lose the woman about whom he holds such extreme views. But he does make his choice, saying, "I had to decide without consulting you." Later, with "evident dread," he asks, "And now, is it all over between us?" But the man's soul is his own, although he does not call it his own. He says of his business proposition:

> It is not the sale of my soul that troubles me: I have sold it too often to care about that. I have sold it for a professorship. I have sold it for an income. I have sold it to escape being imprisoned for refusing to pay taxes for hangmen's ropes and unjust wars and things that I abhor.

Considering all this, it is a remarkable tribute that he should not have sold his soul for Barbara. Clearly, he is not a man to be tyrannized, for all his infatuation, nor is she any kind of a tyrant. Here, and elsewhere in Shaw, the implication is that the more freedom and strength a woman has, the less domineering she will be.

Here the two thematic elements in the play merge. Socialism and feminism move to the same kind of social dynamic. Pernicious alternatives can lead only to a pernicious choice. Women in a state of slavery and men in a state of poverty must make a private choice that saves the self, and any critic must morally approve that choice, whatever pieties it may seem to contravene. Our horror at selling the body or selling the soul must be translated into social terms, remembering always that Shaw deplores the individual gesture of protest or, at least in theory, the individual gesture of charity. The whole basis of society must be revolutionized to make the world fit for humanity. The foundling then need not choose between becoming the next Undershaft and becoming another Peter Shirley, worthless to society and himself except as an interchangeable unit, and often, as here, a pure liability to both. A woman would not have to choose between death in the white lead factory and being, as Shaw politely puts it, "a jewelled vamp" or, in the upper classes, between being an unpleasantly overbearing mammoth and an even more unpleasantly submissive mite. In any case, capitalism and inequality are condemned as much by the loathesomeness of their successes as by the pathos of their failures.

The successes of Andrew Undershaft may seem to deny all this and do confuse the interpretation of the play unless they are sorted out from other ideas of Shaw's, chiefly the idea that some people are natural bosses and will achieve power in any setting, whether the factory, the government, the sweatshop or the brothel. These views are expatiated upon in the prefaces to *The Millionairess* and *The Apple Cart* and elsewhere. In these plays the heiress in one and the king in the other are stripped of the advantages with which they begin, after which they go on to demonstate Shaw's thesis by rising to power again through their own executive abilities. The Shavian boss is not entirely distinct from the vital genius, except that she (or he, as the case may be) adds managing ability to natural vitality. Rare, but never quite clear, cases like Eliza Doolittle in *Pygmalion* may have vital genius without being natural bosses. But the bosses run through Shaw's work in a long comforting line that includes Caesar, Saint Joan, Mrs. Warren, Lina Szczepanowska, Epifania Ognisanti di Parerga, King Magnus, and our own man Undershaft. They can save humanity from the perils of democracy, the perils of chaos and ineffectuality. But, even though Undershaft is one of this perhaps saving remnant, and even though the author's admiration for such men colors the portrait, that does not change the meaning of capitalism in the play. When Shaw condemned democracy, he was far from condoning oligarchy. The two go together in his polemics as they have in fact. Shaw's attacks on "freedom" or in his terms, anarchy, are in essence attacks on free enterprise or, in his terms, economic anarchy. And the apologists for laissez-faire capitalism prove the correctness of this approach by making the same combination in reverse, treating limitations on free enterprise as limitations on personal freedom. So the successes of Undershaft, as a man and as a character, prove exactly nothing about the value of millionaires. Dominators will rise to dominate under any system, and "Communism is the fairy godmother who can transform Bosses into 'servants to all the rest'; but only a creed of Creative Evolution can set the souls of the people free." As is usual in Shaw, all ideas work together, but in a work of art there must be a center. In his "Preface on Bosses," Shaw says, "But private property is not the subject of my demonstration in The Millionairess." The reverse is true of *Major Barbara*. Private property *is* the subject of his demonstration; bosses are not: they are merely one instrument in the service of the idea that private property must go, and with it all the sham and all the cant disguising its hideous realities.

These changes in emphasis may be confusing, but we know that Shaw did not write for schools or schoolteachers and dreaded the day (now fully dawned) when he would be forced on students as required reading. He conceived each play as a piece of dramatic art, a piece for the theater, although powerfully aware of drama as "demonstration." He did not forget the function of bosses in writing *Major Barbara* or deny his socialism in *The Millionairess*, but each has its emphasis. There is a special emphasis also in Undershaft's remarks on warfare. Although he is as plausible as the devil who represents worldly wisdom in *Man and Superman*, he is not merely a devil's advocate. The content of the two speeches that follow is very much the same, but the context is so different that in one instance a truth is being used to defeat the human spirit, and in the other that same truth is one of its triumphs. In the third act of *Man and Superman*, the Devil says:

> In a battle two bodies of men shoot at one another with bullets and explosive shells until one body runs away, when the others chase the fugitives on horseback and cut them to pieces as they fly. And this, the chronicle concludes, shews the greatness an majesty of empires, and the littleness of the vanquished. Over such battles the people run about the streets yelling with delight, and egg their Governments on to spend hundreds of millions of money in the slaughter, whilst the strongest Ministers dare not spend an extra penny in the pound against the poverty and pestilence through which they themselves daily walk. I could give you a thousand instances; but they all come to the same thing: the power that governs the earth is not the power of Life but of Death; and the inner need that has nerved Life to the effort of organizing itself into the human being is not the need for higher life but for a more efficient engine of destruction.

These lines, which resound with appalling relevance in the nuclear age, are answered in their own context by Don Juan, representative of the

Life Force, who does not deny their truth, but does recognize their
devilishness and their partiality. Certainly their cynicism, like all cynicism ultimately, is devilish, but the same does not hold true for
Undershaft's similar remarks in *Major Barbara*. It will not do to forget
that the subject of the colloquy in hell is, naturally, the nature of man,
whereas Undershaft's subject, as we shall see, is the nature of war.
And in complaining about the nature of man, it is only reasonable to
note his unreasonable expenditures on death. But the Devil is by
implication taunting mankind for engaging in warfare at all, while
Undershaft is getting at a somewhat different question, central to the
ideas of the play: the illusions with which society drapes the obscene
limbs of war, illusions expressed in our own time by such euphemisms
as "clean bomb" and "tactical nuclear weapons," and "pacification." A
fool like Lomax assumes that conversation with a maker of cannons
calls for a mealy mouth: "Well, the more destructive war becomes,
the sooner it will be abolished, eh?" Undershaft answers:

> Not at all. The more destructive war becomes the more
> fascinating we find it. No, Mr. Lomax: I am obliged to you
> for making the usual excuse for my trade; but I am not
> ashamed of it. I am not one of those men who keep their
> morals and their business in watertight compartments. All
> the spare money my trade rivals spend on hospitals, cathe-
> drals, and other receptacles for conscience money, I devote
> to experiments and researches in improved methods of de-
> stroying life and property. I have always done so; and I
> always shall.

But Undershaft, though diabolonian in one sense, is not excluding, as
the Devil does, all other human values. He says a moment later: "For
me there is only one true morality; but it might not fit you, as you do
not manufacture aerial battleships. There is only one true morality for
every man; but every man has not the same true morality." This is
not a man who celebrates murder, merely a realist who calls it by its
true name. If his realism makes us shudder, that is intended to make us
shudder at the size of the "defense" budget, at the work going forward
daily on ABC Warfare, at the truth itself, not at Undershaft. That he
should be the form in which the Life Force triumphs under our present
system is in fact our tragedy.

And even if there were any doubt about the meaning of the great
final triumph which sweeps along every member of the family in a

degree of commitment and comprehension exactly tailored to his dramatic figure, there could be no mistake about the meaning of the failures. Poverty *is* a crime: one that fits, with only a little Machiavellianism in the logic, any working definition of the terms. If crime is an action that harms other people or the state, then the crime of poverty is enunciated in the Jeremiad aleady quoted on the subject of "Let Him Be Poor." If crime is that which society punishes, then poverty is a crime. (Logicians are asked to sympathize *pro tem* with Shaw's preference for strict truth over strict logic.) It would take no particular ingenuity to show that the poor are daily and hourly punished as no enlightened state would punish any criminal. Shaw's debt to Butler and Bellamy in this matter is no secret. The pitch of persuasiveness to which he raises the idea is his own.

Besides being based on the same kind of social dynamic, Shaw's socialism and his feminism merge in another and more significant way in *Major Barbara*. As I said earlier, there are three religions in this play. Just as in *Saint Joan*, two religions grapple for the heroine's soul. Catholicism and Protestantism are so mighty, with all the secular issues weighting them both, that Joan is crushed between them. The religions that fight for Barbara's soul are quite another matter. The Salvation Army, in spite of Shaw's faint praise in the preface, is no match for St. Andrew Undershaft. His creed is simple: "My religion? Well, my dear. I am a millionaire. That is my religion." This is to say: I am a materialist and a realist. He has seen and understood the reality that Barbara at last understands when she says:

> Undershaft and Bodger; their hands stretch everywhere: when we feed a starving fellow creature, it is with their bread, because there is no other bread; when we tend the sick, it is in the hospitals they endow; if we turn from the churches they build, we must kneel on the stones of the streets they pave. As long as that lasts, there is no getting away from them. Turning our backs on Bodger and Undershaft is turning our backs on life.

When she has seen the benefits of millionairism as well as the bitterness of the bread of charity, she grows even more dithyrambic:

> it was really all the human souls to be saved; not weak souls in starved bodies, sobbing with gratitude for a scrap of bread and treacle, but fullfed, quarrelsome, snobbish, uppish crea-

Highland Park Public Library

tures, all standing on their little rights and dignities, and thinking that my father ought to be greatly obliged to them for making so much money for him—and so he ought. That is where salvation is really wanted. My father shall never throw it in my teeth again that my converts were bribed with bread. . . . I have got rid of the bribe of bread. I have got rid of the bribe of heaven. Let God's work be done for its own sake; the work he had to create us to do because it cannot be done except by living men and women. When I die, let him be in my debt, not I in his; and let me forgive him as becomes a woman of my rank.

In a play that ends (almost) on this note, Christianity may be vanquished, but materialism has not triumphed, except in the sense that a millionaire has been needed—and a millionaire who makes that his religion is clearly a vital genius—to create a model of socialism. Instead of being crushed between the two forces, Barbara steps from the shaken foundation to the solid one, but the rhythm of the comedy implies that she will go on upward. As the curtain falls she is babbling about a house in the village to live in with her Dolly. The contrast with the ending of *Saint Joan* is instructive. That play ends in bitter sadness, with the question: "Oh God that madest this beautiful earth, when will it be ready to receive Thy saints?" And the implied answer is: Not now; perhaps never. Even taking into account the passage of two decades and a world war, this is more than a historical difference, for Major Barbara is not one of God's saints but one of the saints of this world. It seems possible to infer that the world must be saved by worldly means, that innocence cannot carry us through, but intellect and will power may. And will power must be backed up by fire power. Therefore this play needs no epilogue. Its last lines explode forward into an essentially new future. Barbara drags her mother off to pick out a house in the village, and Undershaft orders his new son-in-law to report for work: "Six o'clock tomorrow morning, Euripides." Two things are certain. Babies are certain, babies blessed with a mother who cares about human souls. This is not a guess. The Life Force means business, not pleasure. And guns for the revolution are almost a certainty. If we read them as standing for all the power that "can destroy the higher powers just as a tiger can destroy a man," then it becomes certain that guns are the tool of revolution no less than the tool of oppression. Disinterested intellect dare not leave the world to the vested interests. This was sometimes a platitude, but now the time gives it teeth. The hope is classic, then. Bigger and better babies, and power on the side of life instead of death.

> Plato says, my friend, that society cannot be saved until either the Professors of Greek take to making gunpowder, or else the makers of gunpowder become Professors of Greek.

Major Barbara is Shaw's Republic of saints.

Shaw's Comedy and *Major Barbara*

William G. McCollom

Shaw once remarked that if he tried to explain his plays to his confused public, they would be ten times more confused. Of course he did explain them, often with misleading effect. If his plays were as intellectually haughty and uncompromising as his prefaces, essays, and statements to the press, he would be remembered primarily as a satirist, not as a comic dramatist. Despite the trumpet blasts introducing his comedy, the plays themselves, no mere expositions of his contempt for error and folly, prove that he was continually seduced by the absurdity of the human spectacle.

In 1897, Shaw reviewed George Meredith's *Essay on Comedy* when it appeared in book form, twenty years after the lecture on which it was based. The occasion was rich in ironic comedy. What would the impossible Irishman, the socialist author of a half-dozen plays including *Mrs. Warren's Profession* and *The Devil's Disciple*, have to say about this refined presentation of comedy as an essentially conservative art reflecting the common sense of a civilized society? What would he think of Meredith's Comic Spirit poised over the heads of congregated ladies and gentlemen, instructing them so nicely about vanity and affectation that they are ready, on signal, to smile with unequalled politeness or break into silvery laughter? Shaw's response was disingenuous in the extreme. The *Essay* is "perfectly straightforward and accurate," as one would expect from "perhaps the highest living au-

From *The Divine Average: A View of Comedy.* © 1971 by the Press of Case Western Reserve University.

thority" on the subject. It is "excellent," "superfine." Yes, but in thinking that the English are capable of appreciating comedy, Mr. Meredith shows that he is as ill-informed about the English public as he is well-informed about comedy. In Shaw's view, English habits, morals, and society completely lack Meredith's common sense. And after twenty years the high authority might perhaps admit that the purpose of comedy is "nothing less than the destruction of old-established morals." Almost fifty years later in *Everybody's Political What's What* Shaw would say during the course of an argument against universal suffrage that mankind is permanently divided into the average, the superaverage, and the subaverage. In the review, only the elite have common sense.

Shaw's revolutionary view of comedy carries over into the *Prefaces*. His high-powered polemics over *Arms and the Man* (1894) might lead one to suppose that the play was as shocking as Ibsen's *Ghosts*. The preface to *Plays Pleasant* (1898) declares that Shaw has been "making war" on the majority of the theatregoing public. A "general onslaught on idealism . . . is implicit, and indeed explicit, in *Arms and the Man* and the naturalist plays of the modern school." The author can no longer accept a morality "shedding fictitious glory on robbery, starvation, disease, crime, drink, war," etc., etc. From such intonations one would think that the witty and genial farce of Raina and Bluntschli must be closer to *The Weavers* than to *The Importance of Being Earnest*. Actually, Wilde's play has more satiric thrust than Shaw's. Satire rarely exorcises the evils it uncovers, but in *Arms and the Man*, Raina and Sergius see through their own romantic sins long before the play is over. Shaw is writing light comedy.

His plays of the new century are, of course, far more serious than *Arms and the Man*. His statement in the review of Meredith that comedy is "the fine art of disillusion," begins to mean not only that comedy supplants childish dreams with mature awareness but that this awareness contains an element of stoic and perhaps ineradicable sadness. Between 1901 and 1905 Shaw wrote *Man and Superman, John Bull's Other Island,* and *Major Barbara*. Each play treats folly and illusion in a distinctive way. Despite its length and its panoply of biological and sociological argument, *Man and Superman* is the most cheerful, even youthful, of the three plays. Yet it reveals increasing maturity in that the archetypal Shavian, John Tanner, instead of carrying everything before him with his cascading speeches, convinces no one, except of his brilliance, repeatedly looks very foolish, and is victimized by a heroine without a single aim beyond that of trapping the man of her choice. In his weaker plays, Shaw sometimes gives the impression that to live the good life, the one thing required is to put your enthymemes in order; but not so here. If Tanner attains a happy ending, it is not because his intelligence has made the right choices but because someone else knows what is right for him.

The play is subtitled "A Comedy and a Philosophy." Apart from the Epistle Dedicatory and the appended Revolutionist's Handbook, the philosophy appears mainly in Tanner's dream during act 3. Although this dream is usually omitted in performance and makes an excellent dialogue in itself, it has important structural significance; for Tanner is suspiciously though entertainingly glib in his waking hours, but in his dream he triumphantly refutes the devil himself in speeches which not only eulogize but seem to embody "the philosophic man: he who seeks in contemplation to discover the inner will of the world, in invention to discover the means of fulfilling that will, and in action to do that will by the so-discovered means." The Doña Ana of his dreams is utterly convinced that such a man must be brought to life; the Ann Whitefield of his waking hours, hearing his final essay in comic desperation, tells him to "go on talking." Only in his dreams is this Shavian hero the stepping-stone to definitely higher things.

Like Larry Doyle in *John Bull's Other Island*, Tanner is both foolish and clever—a good prescription for a comic hero. But there are no heroes in *John Bull*. Neither a comedy nor a tragicomedy nor even a satire, though abundantly satiric, it is a deeply ironic work, perhaps the most bitter and melancholy play Shaw ever wrote. It explores a fundamentally hopeless situation, the relationship of England and Ireland in the early twentieth century. Both countries are to blame for the poverty of Ireland—or rather, two kinds of character are at fault, here the English and the Irish. Although there is a plot, it has little importance. Shaw develops his theme chiefly by means of three characters arranged in hierarchical order. Tom Broadbent, the Gladstonized Englishman, earnest, moral, putting his morality at the service of his interests but completely without hypocrisy, "clever in [his] foolishness," will exploit the Irish with the best will in the world. He will lend them more money on their properties than they are worth, then foreclose his mortgages and appropriate the land for the syndicate he represents. As if this were not enough, he wins an Irish girl with a small fortune and is certain to be elected as an Irish member of the British Parliament, for as a Liberal he favors Home Rule. In his lack of Shaw's "completer consciousness," he is farcical, but ultimately the joke is on Ireland and the poor. His business partner and friend, Larry Doyle, Anglicized Irishman, far more conscious than Broadbent but bitter, cynical, ambivalent in his feelings toward his country because of his tortured wish to escape Irish poverty and footlessness, "foolish in his cleverness," will satirize his friend's blindness but join with him in taking the profits from the land, hating himself for doing so. Mr. Keegan, saint and unfrocked priest under the influence of Oriental philosophy, neither foolish nor merely clever, clearly sees the condition of Ireland, understands what is ruining her, arraigns her betrayers, and dreams of a religious Utopia.

The Broadbents and the Doyles control Ireland for the present, but, if Keegan is right, "the day may come when these islands shall live by the quality of their men rather than by the abundance of their minerals." This tentative statement comes closer to hope than any other in the play. In the powerful final scene Keegan's vision of Ireland merges with the heaven he would substitute for the hell of modern life. When Broadbent asks what this heaven is like, Keegan answers that it is a commonwealth in which Church, State, and people are one. "It is a temple in which the priest is the worshipper and the worshipper the worshipped: three in one and one in three. It is a godhead in which all life is human and all humanity divine: three in one and one in three. It is, in short, the dream of a madman." The dream is clearly related to the vitalist aspirations of Shaw, but here it is the vision of a mystic whom everyone tolerates but ignores. Compared with Tanner's dreams, Keegan's are utterly lacking in cocksureness and so far more moving. In comedy the divine average is triumphant. One measure of the distance between comedy and *John Bull* is that in Shaw's play this triumph seems very far away, so distant as to be almost inconceivable.

The follies and illusions at which Shaw laughs are the subject matter of his comedies. Sometimes these follies and illusions are eradicable, as in *Arms and the Man*, sometimes not, as in *Getting Married*, which presents marriage as absurd but unavoidable and finally tolerable. But there are follies which he regards as disastrous. Characteristically, he does not treat these as the errors of tragic heroes; despite *Saint Joan*, perhaps the tragic hero is the one paradox in which he did not believe. "Tragic" error is social, not personal, as one may see in *John Bull* and *Heartbreak House*. In the Irish play, the men selected to represent Ireland's destroyers are ridiculous or pitiful, and the only man with the brains and the desire to save her is helpless. In *Heartbreak House*, Captain Shotover, who speaks for Shaw, inveighs against the generations who have followed him, but their representatives onstage are delightful or amusing or both. Shaw's darker plays tend to be ironic rather than tragic or tragicomic.

In *John Bull*, the gap between Broadbent and the meaning of what he is doing threatens to scatter the play into fragments. In *Major Barbara*, a more dramatic play, there is a strong tension between the comedy of its people and what Shaw takes to be the intolerable state of modern society, but the strain is not excessive. The total effect is that of problem comedy. If Barbara and Cusins had rejected Undershaft's invitation to join the firm of Undershaft and Lazarus and had lapsed into hopelessness, the play would have been predominantly ironic. As concluded, it offers a hopeful, though hypothetical, solution to the problem posed.

Major Barbara contains a plot within an allegory. The central question of the plot is this: who shall succeed Andrew Undershaft as director of Undershaft and Lazarus, munitions makers? Symbolically considered, the question means: what shall replace the ruinous state of modern civilization, in which men have to choose among poverty, crime, and prosperity built on war and legalized theft?

Lady Britomart Undershaft, daughter of the Earl of Stevenage, naturally thinks that her son Stephen (crown) should inherit his father's industrial empire, which is so powerful that its products are purchased by foreign nations through loans floated by the British government. Like Spenser's Britomart, she is clad in unassailable virtue—"ne euill thing she fear'd, ne euill thing she ment." But Undershaft is determined to follow the tradition of his firm that a foundling always inherits the business. Besides, Stephen in incompetent. Though Shaw was an aristocratic socialist who demanded equal distribution of wealth while denying the ability of many or most men to choose their leaders intelligently, he obviously thought that the ruling classes in England had failed. Leaders might emerge from any class. The Liberal aristocrats are as bad as the Conservatives, if not worse. One recalls that the ridiculous Broadbent in *John Bull's Other Island* was a fervent Liberal. Lady Brit is proud of her Whig background and, like Roebuck Ramsden in *Man and Superman*, has a library from which advanced books are not excluded. At one point Stephen picks up a copy of a Liberal weekly. But Liberalism is not enough.

Undershaft becomes strongly attracted to his vital daughter, Major Barbara of the Salvation Army, and decides to convert her to his own religion, which he first announces as money and gunpowder but later reveals as vitalist, with at least a touch of the Dionysian. He is also drawn to Barbara's fiancé, Adolphus Cusins, a Greek professor and collector of religions, including the Dionysian. Cusins's first name means "noble wolf," and Shaw said he had chosen the character's name carefully. His family name is a function of the plot, for when he learns that only a foundling can inherit the firm, he reveals that his mother was his father's deceased wife's sister—which in Lady Brit's interpretation makes him his own cousin. This farcical development illustrates Shaw's method of placing in comic perspective ideas about which he felt the deepest concern. It is as if he needed to keep them at a distance, so strongly did they shake him.

Undershaft is a realist-mystic. Cusins and Barbara are humanitarian idealists, both ignorant of economic and political realities. Their education or conversion is necessary to the happy ending. And conversion of superior people like them is necessary to the Utopia envisioned by Shaw. But the full meaning of this conversion can be understood only by consideration of the play in some detail.

Each of the four divisions of the play opens with deceptively amusing dialogue and moves toward more overtly serious conflict. If the tone of the opening scene in Lady Brit's library had been preserved throughout the comedy, the work could bear Wilde's ironic subtitle for *The Importance of Being Earnest*—"A Trivial Comedy for Serious People." Just as Wilde's criticism of private property, private charity, the Church, and the press, as voiced in "The Soul of Man under Socialism" (1891), reappears in *The Importance of Being Earnest*, so Shaw's themes emerge in his first act, though wearing the guise of drawing-room comedy. The scene is masterful both as exposition and for its characterization of Lady Britomart, at once so strong-minded and so immersed in the illusions that she and her class know what is right and who should rule the world. The presentation of these illusions adumbrates Shaw's attempt, in later scenes, at transvaluation of values, his demand for a new concept of crime and punishment, and his call for a new aristocracy.

As the play proceeds, Lady Brit quickly loses her dominating position. Unlike Lady Bracknell, Wilde's social juggernaut, Lady Brit has been adjusted to a dramatic world in which real conflicts and hesitations are possible. She can easily control Sarah Undershaft and her clownish fiancé, Lomax—tag ends of the aristocratic tradition. But the immature Stephen insists on growing up. Barbara and Cusins are stronger than she and hopeful symbols for the future of England. Their poise can be seen in such small details as Cusins's ironic statement to Lady Brit, "You have my unhesitating support in everything you do," and even in Barbara's cool way of responding to a belligerent question from her mother by sitting on a table and whistling "Onward, Christian Soldiers."

Soon after the family assembles, Undershaft arrives in response to Lady Brit's summons, for she has some requests to make of her estranged husband. At his entrance, Undershaft is described as "on the surface" an easygoing man, kindly, patient, and simple. "His gentleness is partly that of a strong man who has learned by experience that his natural grip hurts ordinary people." Although Shaw's characters do not always live up to their advance billing, this sentence should be remembered while Undershaft is making the sensational speeches that seem to exhibit utter indifference to suffering and death. It is essential to the effect of the play that he should postpone as long as possible any admission of humane sentiments, for a main point of the comedy is that these feelings will have to be shelved if the world is to emerge from the inferno of the twentieth century.

In 1905, Japan defeated Russia in the Far East, and the Revolution of 1905, was the first major blow to absolute monarchy in Russia. This revolution is on Shaw's mind when he writes in his Preface: "I am and always have been, and shall now always be, a revolutionary writer. . . . Our natural safety from the cheap and devastating explosives which every Russian student can make, and every Russian grenadier has learnt to handle in Manchuria, lies in the fact that brave and resolute men, when they are rascals, will not risk their skins for the good of humanity, and, when they are not, are sympathetic enough to care for humanity, abhorring murder, and never committing it until their consciences are outraged beyond endurance." Brave and resolute men had not shrunk from murder in Russia. How long would they continue to do so in England?

Undershaft is not a Communist. He is a business man who blows up soldiers through intermediaries, and at a huge profit. In the first act, after some preliminary farce which establishes him as likely prone to mistaking identities, he announces his first position on the morality of war production. The greater the success his engineers have in increasing the destructiveness of his weapons, the more "amiable" he becomes. So he says, and no one, except Lomax, begs leave to find a justification for this good humor. Far from being ashamed of his business, far from salving his conscience by huge gifts to charity, he wishes to be distinguished from rivals "who keep their morals and their business in water-tight compartments." His morality is a function of his work, and for him the moral course is to put back into his industry what others sacrifice to charity.

But even in the first act, the audience may become suspicious of so much villainy in so pleasant a man. What are his real motives? He gives no evidence of wanting great wealth or power for himself. To say that he merely enjoys shocking conventional people is no answer; he has something else on his mind. The more shamelessly he plays out—and plays up—his role as ruthless capitalist, the more shameful modern capitalism appears. The capitalists are the power-structure, and Undershaft admires power. But when placed beside his object-lesson in shamelessness, this admiration leads to the thought that power is in the wrong hands. Can Undershaft be holding power as trustee for a beneficiary that has not yet appeared? Who is the found-ling to be?

The Barbara-theme is sounded next. When Stephen divides humanity into honest men and scoundrels, Barbara replies that all are sinners but none are scoundrels. Salvation by faith awaits them all. Undershaft wants to know if even a maker of cannons may be saved. The question leads to a contract. If he will come to her Salvation Army shelter, she will visit his cannon works. Each will attempt to "save" the other. Now the bargain will be sealed by a religious service. As all reject Lady Brit's demand for Anglican prayers, her power begins to crumble.

Act 2, in the West Ham shelter, puts in action the vigorous, devoted, but misapplied leadership of Barbara in the struggle to raise the depressed classes. The act succeeds in being both an entertaining genre picture and a comprehensive attack on current social conditions. The recipients of charity show far greater knowledge of the world than do the naive Salvation Army workers. The system drags down men with brains and ability, and for all its good will, the Army cannot accomplish much. An intelligent object of charity almost sums up the act when he says to Barbara: "Ah! it's a pity you never was trained to use your reason, miss. Youd have been a very taking lecturer on Secularism." Barbara is at her strongest in her battle for the soul of Bill Walker, a brute who has just struck a Salvation Army girl in the face. Barbara's friendly, courageous manner awakens in him the remorse that she hopes will lead him to God. But Undershaft arrives at the shelter.

In an important scene between Undershaft and Cusins, the two men agree that the spirit of God is more important than his name. Convinced that this spirit is within Barbara—a handsome example of what the evolutionary process can accomplish—Undershaft resolves to turn her propagation of faith from God to gunpowder. Excited by his idea, he declares, "I shall hand on my torch to my daughter. She shall make my converts and preach my gospel—." At the moment of utterance, this prediction sounds like mere perversity or madness, but as the scene moves on, the inner meaning of this Dionysus-Machiavelli becomes clearer. To Cusins he says with ostentatious harshness, "What have we three to do with the common mob of slaves and idolaters?" The Shaw-Undershaft mind is so rapt in a vision not yet defined that the speaker can coolly ignore the poor souls at his feet. And it is helpful to remember that much of Shaw's life was devoted to improving the lot of people for whom, as individuals, he had a low regard. He will not love the common people until they have been made uncommon by present standards. In a major speech attacking poverty Undershaft says, "We three must stand together above the common people: how else can we help their children to climb up beside us?" If the older generation is already beyond salvation, the men of the future are not. The way must be prepared by shattering Barbara's faith in the God of charity and passivity. Undershaft will accomplish this feat by showing her that the Army must depend on the contributions of those whose lives are devoted to destroying its ideals.

When Cusins points out that the Army makes men sober, honest, unselfish, and spiritual, his mentor replies that these qualities are safeguards against socialism and revolution and therefore pleasing to him as an industrialist. Taken literally, his argument here is inconsistent with the higher motives he elsewhere intimates. But for the moment he is speaking not as himself but as The Capitalist, and giving Cusins an elementary lesson in political economy.

In the last section of this act, Barbara almost succeeds in her fight for Bill Walker. She will not allow him to pay for his blow by inviting another or by giving money. Baffled, he seems ready to accept religion and repentance. But word comes that a prominent distiller is offering £5,000 to the Salvation Army. Despite Barbara's horror, the Army will gratefully accept. Bill relapses into cynicism with his memorable question, "Wot prawce selvytion nah?" Barbara's occupation is gone.

Shaw did not like to be dismissed as brilliant, but apart from some brilliant light comedy, the first scene in act 3 is mainly an opportunity for a big speech by Undershaft instructing the fatuous Stephen that capital, not Parliament, rules the country. The government recognizes capital's needs as national needs and is ready to call out the police when private enterprise is threatened. This is one of Undershaft's more ruthless moments, for there is no point in his explaining to Stephen what is really on his mind. Even if Undershaft unmasked, Stephen could not understand him.

The final scene takes place at Perivale St. Andrews, on a height looking down on the beautiful community built by Undershaft. The name of the place, its elevation, and its beauty help to give Andrew Undershaft the religious status he asserts in tones not merely ironical. Manufacturing death, the workers live a good life. The chief question of the scene is whether Cusins, greatly tempted by the place, can bridge the moral abyss between himself and Undershaft. He does so by a process of reasoning largely supplied by Undershaft. As if to show how difficult the decision to join him will be, Undershaft quickly reasserts his ruthlessness: he takes pleasure in the destructiveness of his weapons but remains indifferent to the identity of the victor in the wars of the time. He will sell arms to anyone who will pay for them. But in his oblique way, he reveals two justifications for this policy. First, it has enabled him to build a town which a sane society could study with profit. Secondly, his amorality is a goad applied to the flanks of the timid. Poverty and slavery, he says, can be destroyed by bullets. "If you good people prefer preaching and shirking to buying my weapons and fighting the rascals, dont blame me." Money and power are prerequisite to good deeds. And as Cusins still wavers, Shaw's Machiavelli speaks more pointedly: "Whatever can blow men up can blow society up."

Cusins is moving to the acknowledgment that power is the basis of social change for good or evil. But he clings to the Christian virtues of love and pity. He is in the dilemma of the Fabian socialist torn between "gradualness" and violent revolution. When he says that he hates war, Undershaft replies, "Hatred is the coward's revenge for being intimidated. Dare you make war on war?" He can go no further without destroying his persona as war profiteer.

Alone with Barbara, Cusins announces his decision to accept Undershaft's dare—for that is what it is. Undershaft has offered power. Cusins will ultimately use it not indifferently but for the common good. Intellectual, imaginative, and religious power, he now declares, have served the few against the many; his guns will create a counterforce. He has already said that he will choose his clients, though Undershaft has forbidden such a course. Adolphus can one day become the "noble wolf" suggested by his name. By such a course he would "cozen" the forces of darkness. The audience may wonder just how Cusins will be able to use his factory for the common people, but Shaw cannot answer that question within the play without acts or plans instituting revolution. This would jeopardize the comedy.

The Greeks considered all who did not speak their language "barbarians," Gentiles outside the law. Barbara ceases to be a barbarian. She too is converted by her tour of Perivale St. Andrews and by her indoctrination in the "Gospel of St. Andrew Undershaft." "Transfigured," she says, "I have got rid of the bribe of bread. I have got rid of the bribe of heaven." She will help to unveil "an eternal light in the Valley of the Shadow." We are to believe that the *élan vital* of the daughter is not less than that of her "mystic" father. She will place her spiritual gift at the service of men not irretrievably shackled by poverty but free to advance in human godliness.

The ironic method of Undershaft has educated Cusins and Barbara. The other members of the family group are beyond "salvation" and remain variously foolish. Lomax is at the bottom of the hierarchy, though like certain Restoration fools, he at one point stumbles on the "truth" as he says: "The fact is, you know, there's a certain amount of tosh about this notion of wickedness. It doesnt work. . . . You see, all sorts of chaps are always doing all sorts of things; and we have to fit them in somehow, dont you know." Sarah has nothing on her mind. Stephen begins with a perfectly conventional horror of Undershaft. He learns to admire his father's business acumen but is incapable of learning much more than that. He will continue to suffer from the illusions of the unthinking members of his class. Lady Brit, for all her absurd narrowness, wins respect for her formidable strong-mindedness. She proves that Shaw can clearly distinguish between illusion and the illuded but attractive personality.

The decision to cure Barbara of her illusions and to give her a credible faith was daring, but it did not succeed. She is the great disappointment of the play. Shaw could not find the vocabulary for her new religion. In the early scenes it is piquant that so charming and lively a girl should be speaking the naive language of the Salvation Army. Her verve seems to justify her simple notions, though what she actually says can command little more than smiling sympathy. But from the moment of her disillusionment and defeat at the West Ham shelter, Shaw does not quite know what to do with her. At the first production in 1905, some reviewers were scandalized by the moment in which, "almost delirious," she cries. "My God: why hast thou forsaken me?" The line is objectionable not because it is blasphemous but because it is out of key with the character and the context. Inevitably, the words suggest either that Barbara is of very great stature or that her conception of her own role is vastly inflated. Yet she is neither a tragic heroine nor a fool.

In the third act, her decision to save the souls of the well-fed and complacent residents of Perivale St. Andrews is accompanied by grandiose rhetoric. To Cusins she exclaims, "Oh! did you think my courage would never come back? did you believe that I was a deserter? that I, who have stood in the streets, and taken my people to my heart, and talked of the holiest and greatest things with them, could ever turn back and chatter foolishly to fashionable people about nothing in a drawing room?" It is not at all clear that Undershaft's employees will need to be taken to her heart. And when she adds, "Oh! and I have my dear little Dolly boy still," one would expect the Greek professor to be slightly embarrassed. Barbara sounds more foolish after salvation than before. One may conclude that she has exchanged one illusion for another.

Cusins makes his transitions more successfully, in part because he has not been committed to an untenable position. In act 2 Undershaft stuns him by demolishing standard and comforting ideas; in the third act the professor begins to think for himself. He has been called the protagonist of the play, but this is to make too much of conclusions almost put in his mouth by Undershaft. Near the beginning of the last scene he says that if he had been interested in power he would not have come to the munitions plant, yet at the close he wants to accept power for all. Alone with Barbara, he says, "I love the common people," opposing the stated scorn of Undershaft. "I want to arm them against the lawyers, the doctors, the priests, the literary men, the professors, the artists, and the politicians, who, once in authority, are more disastrous and tyrannical than all the fools, rascals, and impostors." This dazzling Shavian hyperbole makes Cusins sound like Undershaft even as he propounds ideas that Undershaft could not explicitly accept. Cusins is walking a logical tightrope, taking suggestions from his teacher and pushing them to previously unexpressed conclusions. There may be some doubt whether he would say all this to Undershaft, but even if the passage is not fully adjusted to the context, it is morally and theatrically plausible.

Most of the minor characters show no strain between life and idea. Lady Brit, for example, is wholly consistent and delightfully real. Barbara and Cusins have to struggle with Shaw's plans for them. But Undershaft is the great achievement of the play. Like John Tanner he is a prodigious talker, but whereas Tanner is transparent, Undershaft has about him the mystery of a poetic creation. He seems to be all compact of oratory, but as we listen to him moving from brutal advocacy of warmaking to his last significant question, "Dare you make war on war?" we begin to attribute to him an inner conflict which is not presented psychologically. He remains a mask, but increasingly we are aware of the face beneath. He is a character whose whereabouts can be plotted though it is not seen by the naked eye.

Ultimately we realize that he regards himself as custodian of power held ready for one who will use it rightly—though his profession forbids him to use that adverb. One hint of his inner meaning is contained in the aphorism he assigns to the Undershaft who preceded him: "NOTHING IS EVER DONE IN THIS WORLD UNTIL MEN ARE PREPARED TO KILL ONE ANOTHER IF IT IS NOT DONE." Scoundrels have no objection to violence, but the point is that the victims of oppression must prepare to turn on their oppressors. Undershaft's "realism" does not exclude Shaw's intense moral feeling. In addition to being a Dionysus and a Machiavelli, he is also a Moses who cannot enter the Promised Land.

His complex passion is projected in speeches which, at first restrained, rise to torrential force. When Mrs. Baines tells him that although the Army fights drunkenness, the distiller Saxmunden is making a large gift to the Army, Undershaft tears out the check he has just signed and says to her:

> I also, Mrs. Baines, may claim a little disinterestedness. Think of my business! think of the widows and orphans! the men and lads torn to pieces with shrapnel and poisoned with lyddite! [*Mrs. Baines shrinks; but he goes on remorselessly*] the oceans of blood, not one drop of which is shed in a really just cause! the ravaged crops! the peaceful peasants forced, women and men, to till their fields under the fire of opposing armies on pain of starvation! the bad blood of the fierce little cowards at home who egg on others to fight for the gratification of their national vanity! All this makes money for me: I am never richer, never busier than when the papers

> are full of it. Well, it is your work to preach peace on earth and goodwill to men. [*Mrs. Baines's face lights up again.*] Every convert you make is a vote against war. [*Her lips move in prayer.*] Yet I give you this money to help you to hasten my own commercial ruin. [*He gives her the cheque.*]

One purpose of the speech is to prove to Cusins the thesis that the Army can be bought. A second purpose is to separate Barbara from her faith and work, for Undershaft has already decided that she must preach his gospel. But coming from one who grows rich on war, the words are ignited by irony. They condemn charity from millionaires and, more important, uncover the speaker's conviction that up to 1905, no modern war has been fought for a justifiable reason. We notice that the only kind of war mentioned pits nation against nation. While not abandoning his doctrine of power, the speech reveals through its violent indirection an intense though unspecified desire for revolutionary change. Undershaft means more than he says. Only Cusins has a chance of understanding him.

The speech begins in ominous quiet, rises to a climax of horror, and falls back into the irony with which it began. The long series is a very marked characteristic of Shaw's prose. The series beginning with "my business" contains seven members, not an unusually large number for Shaw in his non-dramatic writing. Undershaft talks much as Shaw writes. As elsewhere in Undershaft's use of series, the members grow progressively longer, flooding the listener with the weight of the speaker's conviction. Only the fifth member interrupts the expansion. The iron-willed force of the speech is increased by another stylistic trait of Shaw, his proneness to total assertions and denials. "Not one" drop of blood has been shed in a just cause. "All this" enriches Undershaft. He is "never" richer or busier than when the newspapers are "full" of war. The horrors are, of course, specific enough; they strike harder through alliteration and balanced phrases. The entire speech resounds with powerful but directed emotion.

In *Major Barbara*, the comic form just succeeds in containing impulses toward violence. Scorn, wrath, Nietzschean contempt for the virtues of forbearance and pity join with a radicalism grown fiercely impatient and encounter a faith in life supported by a quite normal liking for people. The shock of battle is there; a state of high tension persists to the final curtain. For now, comedy holds the stage, but there is no assurance that Shaw will not soon drive it into the wings.

Actually, he was not about to do so. Perhaps his faith in the power of life to raise even the "subaverage" to ever higher levels of consciousness ultimately gripped him more strongly than his long and intense preoccupation with the question: what can now be made of the crooked stick of man? Shaw the Utopian supported Shaw the comic dramatist. His plays extended the boundaries of comedy and were, he must have hoped, a significant moment in the evolution of mankind, for as he made his Father Keegan say in the last scene of *John Bull's Other Island*, "Every jest is an earnest in the womb of Time."

Skeptical Faith

Margery M. Morgan

Major Barbara has been generally acclaimed as one of Shaw's finest plays. The impact it made on Brecht is indicated by the extent to which it inspired *St Joan of the Stockyards*. Francis Fergusson's account of it [in *The Idea of a Theater*] as a "farce of rationalizing," however denigratory in tone, is true to the quicksilver brilliance and buoyancy of the play, as careful analysis cannot be. To attempt such analysis would be misguided if it were not necessary to show that the intellectual intricacy of the dramatic structure is precise, not confused, and that Shaw now handles his ironies with a clarity and control lacking in the comparably ironic *Candida*.

The mainspring of the play seems to have been provided by Shaw's response to Blake, reinforced by a reading of Nietzsche where he is closest to Blake. The dialectical terms of *The Marriage of Heaven and Hell* provide the intellectual perspectives of the drama:

> Without contraries is no progression. Attraction and repulsion, reason and energy, love and hate, are necessary to human existence.

> From these contraries spring what the religions call good and evil. Good is the passive that obeys reason; evil is the active springing from energy.

> Good is heaven. Evil is hell.

From *The Shavian Playground*. ©1972 by Margery M. Morgan. Methuen, 1972.

Conventional moral distinctions are annihilated as the antinomies prove to be complementary. Like *The Marriage of Heaven and Hell, Major Barbara* employs the shock tactics of paradox to induce a more comprehensive understanding of the world. The means used involve insistence on both literal and metaphoric meanings, simple and ironic readings.

Shaw's original intention of calling the play *Andrew Undershaft's Profession* implied the reworking of the pun already employed in *Cashel Byron's Profession* and *Mrs Warren's Profession*, so as to bring out the relation between a trade or occupation and the creed implicit in its pursuit. In each instance (and this also applies to *Widowers' Houses*), practice of the occupation is permitted, or even relied on, by society, while official morality disapproves. On the realistic level, the munitions firm of Undershaft and Lazarus and Bodger's whisky firm represent capitalist enterprise exploiting human weakness for pecuniary gain and producing further social evils, destructive to humanity. In theory, Christians reject war; they are answered by the "Voice of the Devil" (Blake's phrase) issuing from Andrew Undershaft, in whom Blake's view of Satan and Nietzsche's Dionysus unite to form one of Shaw's most impressive characters. Imaginative vision, it seems, can use the devil as a friend who has important truths to tell: gunpowder, fire and drink have positive value as symbols of elemental power, revolutionary, cleansing, inspirational. Indeed they are symbols in the Coleridgean sense, marked by a translucence of the general in the particular and of the eternal in the temporal; they are true symbols of power for change because, as material objects, they can bring about change. Together they represent the general Blakean category of Energy. Shaw associates with them—as society does—money, capitalist profit (or Illth), which can also be positively seen as a token of natural abundance translated into the commodities of civilization and *human* power, which reason can master and wield.

Certainly nowhere else in Shaw's work do we come so close to the imaginative sense of Blake's propositions:

1. Man has no body distinct from his soul . . .
2. Energy is the only life, and is from the body; and reason is the bound or outward circumference of energy . . .

and, above all, the sense of:

3. Energy is eternal delight.

Undershaft, the manufacturer of armaments, is in a different relation to society from Sartorius, the slum landlord of *Widowers' Houses*, or Mrs Warren, owner-director of an international chain of brothels. Whereas those earlier creations remain prisoners of society, outcasts from respectability, and in presentation are touched with the pathos of melodrama, the nature of the commodity Undershaft traffics in puts him in mastery over society and gives him the confidence and author-ity to set up his sign: "UNASHAMED," implying a total rejection of (puritan) guilt on all fronts. In this play Shaw grasped the basic nature of the threat offered to the intellect by the actual world: the challenge of undifferentiated force and mass in the physical universe to the essentially sole and individual; the ruthless and mindless violence that "can destroy the higher power just as a tiger can destroy a man." But man naturally has a tiger in him, too, which can match the violence of the elements. Active, aggressive, this force is translated into social terms under the image of an army. The literal fact of the Salvation Army is essential to the realistic fabric of the play. Traditional meta-phors of Christian life as warfare are already implicit in the uniformed figures of men and women, marching with banners, bearing the sign "Blood and Fire," to a drum that beats out a quickened pulse of life. As interpreted through Cusins, Major Barbara's fiancé, it takes on the more general significance of the Church Militant of a universal reli-gion: organized humanity, active, purposeful and joyous in its on-slaughts against misery and darkness. The play as a whole demonstrates its theme by the physical exhilaration and the optimism it generates through its explosions of condensed thought and the aggressive release of laughter.

As in *Mrs Warren's Profession*, the basic conflict of opposites is again enacted within a child-parent relationship: the innocence of soci-ety's dupes is confronted with the disillusion of its exploiters. But this time the parent and the child are of opposite sexes, and experience does not simply destroy innocence; it complements it and produces new strength. The simple dialectical plan, in which Barbara's heavenly counsel and Undershaft's hellish counsel fight it out, was complicated in the process of writing, when Shaw transformed the heroine's fiancé from a young man-about-town comparable to Charles Lomax (for so he is characterized at the beginning of the longhand version) to a Professor of Greek. I think we can assume that Cusins was at first envisaged as playing a minor, or choric, role comparable to Frank's in the earlier play: that of an observer and commentator who also sets the comic tone of the drama. In his character of observer, the Professor of Greek is qualified to identify for us the philosophical issues and the mythopoetic analogues as they arise. His intellectual quality does not entirely obscure the lineaments of the clown; but he plays the ironical fool to Lomax's "natural." As a more considerable and distinguished member of society, he is also fitted to become one of the main pivots of the dramatic scheme. The extension in the play's significance which has followed from this later conception of the character culminates in a scrap of dialogue inserted as an after-thought in the longhand text of act 3 (B.M. Addit. MS. 50616 A-E).

> UNDERSHAFT: . . . Remember the words of Plato.
>
> CUSINS [*starting*]: Plato! You dare to quote Plato to me!
>
> UNDERSHAFT: Plato says, my friend, that society cannot be saved until either the Professors of Greek take to making gunpowder, or else the makers of gunpowder become Professors of Greek.

To the opposition between Undershaft and Barbara there has been added an independent opposition between Undershaft and Cusins. Of course, these are various examples of a single basic conflict between idealism and realism. But the placing of the two in the progress of the drama must absolve Shaw from any charge of tautology: Barbara, the indubitable protagonist of act 2, subsides into watchfulness in act 3, while Cusins takes over from her, is put to the test and makes the crucial decision; her endorsement of this in the last moments of the play lends strength to the impression that he has indeed been deputizing for her. It is dramatically necessary, after her defeat by Undershaft in act 2, that the initiative should pass from Barbara. Cusins carries the play into its final movement, as he makes his pact with Undershaft. This has the effect of restoring Barbara to her proper centrality, though now in alliance with her former opponents. As the representative of spirituality, she returns to inform and bless the compact between reason and energy and the paradox of good *in* evil, heaven *in* hell. Cusins's function has been to introduce the dialectical synthesis. The reconciliation he proposes between power and service, realism and idealism, corresponds, of course, to the Platonic advocacy of the philosopher-king.

The peculiarly Shavian variety of Ibsenite dramatic structure, imitated from the Platonic dialogues, is evident in the verbal debates, rationally conceived and conducted to a great extent—especially in the last act—in abstract terms. This is the drama of ideas in exemplary form. But there is much more to the play than this. The realism of its settings—the library in Wilton Crescent, the Salvation Army shelter in Canning Town, and the especially topical Garden City—establishes it as a critique of actual society that reveals the spectrum of class and its cruel contrasts, as *Man and Superman* did not. Changes of setting are matched by changes in dramatic style. Wealth, aristocracy and the culture that goes with them play out a comedy of manners in act 1; Dickensian realism verging on melodrama invades act 2, in the Salvation Army Shelter, bare and chill, with its horse-trough as derisive comment on the poorly dressed wretches at their free meal; act 3 presents a Utopia designed by contemporary paternalism, and theory reigns there—a front for the Satanic mills that produce the wealth of Wilton Crescent, or that, differently directed, could blow the whole unequal system sky-high. Metaphysically, Perivale St Andrews represents the spiritual cosmos, heaven and hell and the battlefield of the world (in its fort with dummy soldiers), corresponding to the emotional range—touching tragedy and ecstasy—that the play embraces. The action of *Major Barbara* contains thinly disguised versions of folklore quests and divine rituals, as well as sharp clashes of personality, to set off the philosophy. The dialectical scheme is strongly supported by mythopoetic patterns and humanized by a rich assortment of characters. The second act in particular with its centrally placed subplot, involving Barbara with a character from a subgroup, Bill Walker, is highly exciting in the pace of its symbolically weighted action and the intense sense of crisis it conveys. Energy, one is reminded, is the stuff of drama.

Energy, of course, is the power that Nietzsche called Dionysian and regarded as the antithesis of the Socratic poise he defined as apollonian. "The business of the Salvation Army is to save, not to wrangle about the name of the pathfinder," declares Cusins. "Dionysos or another: what does it matter?" The protest was anticipated by Nietzsche himself in the passage from his preface to *The Birth of Tragedy* already mentioned in relation to *Candida*:

> It was *against* morality, therefore, that my instinct, as an intercessory instinct for life, turned in this questionable book, inventing for itself a fundamental counter-dogma and counter-valuation of life, purely artistic, purely *anti-Christian*. What should I call it? As a philologist and man of words I baptized

it, not without some liberty—for who could be sure of the proper name of the Antichrist?—with the name of a Greek god: I called it *Dionysian*.

In fact, Dionysus is mentioned in the dialogue with sufficient frequency to justify entirely the critics Shaw attacked in his preface for labelling his play as derivative from Nietzschean philosophy. Barbara Undershaft, the evangelist, represents the orthodox Christian attitude that Nietzsche described as "a libel on life." Her father, whom Cusins nicknames "Prince of Darkness" and "Mephistopheles," as well as "Dionysos" and "Machiavelli," challenges her with the "fundamental counter-dogma and counter-valuation of life":

> Leave it to the poor to pretend that poverty is a blessing: leave it to the coward to make a religion of his cowardice by preaching humility;
> I had rather be a thief than a pauper. I had rather be a murderer than a slave.
> I dont want to be either; but if you force the alternative on me, then, by Heaven, I'll choose the braver and more moral one.

In adding to these two the figure of a Professor of Greek, Shaw had supplied his play with a representative of that dispassionate and philosophical Hellenic consciousness upon which Nietzsche saw the originally Asiatic religion of Dionysus as having broken in, at a critical point in the history of civilization. The passage in *The Birth of Tragedy* that supplies the fullest account of this event and its consequences can be related illuminatingly to *Major Barbara*:

> On the other hand, we should not have to speak conjecturally, if asked to disclose the immense gap which separated the *Dionysian Greek* from the Dionysian barbarian.

Already this hints at the rationale of supplying Undershaft with a double opposition in, first, the aptly named Barbara, and then Professor Cusins. The famous essay goes on:

> From all quarters of the Ancient World . . . we can prove the existence of Dionysian festivals, the type of which bears, at best, the same relation to the Greek festivals as the bearded satyr, who borrowed his name and attributes from the goat, does to Dionysus himself . . . the very wildest beasts of

nature were let loose here, including that detestable mixture of lust and cruelty which has always seemed to me the genuine "witches' draught."

Now Shaw has almost entirely dissociated these forces from his principal characters. They are symbolically represented in the play by Undershaft's explosives and the wars in which they are used: "the men and lads torn to pieces with shrapnel and poisoned with lyddite! . . . the oceans of blood . . . the ravaged crops!"—by "Bodger's Whisky in letters of fire against the sky," by the drum that Cusins beats, and by the Salvation Army motto of "Blood and Fire!" More directly, they are present in the physical violence with which Bill Walker disturbs the shelter, in act 2, and for which he has prepared himself by drinking gin:

> Aw'm noa gin drinker . . . ; bat when Aw want to give my girl a bloomin good awdin Aw lawk to ev a bit o devil in me.

Returning to Nietzsche, we find the immunity of Shaw's principal characters, the educated and the aristocratic, accounted for:

> For some time . . . it would seem that the Greeks were perfectly secure and guarded against the feverish agitations of these festivals . . . by the figure of Apollo himself rising here in full pride, who could not have held out the Gorgon's head to a more dangerous power than this grotesquely uncouth Dionysian. It is in Doric art that this majestically-rejecting attitude of Apollo perpetuated itself.

The production note which prepares for Cusins's first entrance on the stage refers to his *"appalling temper."* The character described is that of a man who has obtained mastery over his own passions and thus, according to Socrates, fitted himself for the task of governing others:

> *The lifelong struggle of a benevolent temperament and a high conscience against impulses of inhuman ridicule and fierce impatience has set up a chronic strain. . . . He is a most implacable, determined, tenacious, intolerant person who by mere force of character presents himself as—and indeed actually is— considerate, gentle, explanatory, even mild and apologetic, capable possibly of murder, but not of cruelty or coarseness.*

Cusins has his proper place in Lady Britomart Undershaft's library. Its decorum, reflecting her own majestic rejection of all licence, is an essential adjunct to its perfect security; she is herself prepared to recognize the dependence of the standards of a gentleman upon the tradition of classical education.

The significance of Cusins's crucial decision to accept a directorship in the Undershaft firm, in order to "make war on war," can be explored in terms of the rest of the passage from *The Birth of Tragedy*, which grows now even more closely analogous to the play than in its earlier sentences:

> This opposition became more precarious and even impossible, when, from out of the deepest root of the Hellenic nature, similar impulses finally broke forth and made way for themselves: *the Delphic god, by a seasonably effected reconciliation, was now contented with taking the destructive arms from the hands of his powerful antagonist.* This reconciliation marks the most important moment in the history of the Greek cult: wherever we turn our eyes we may observe the revolutions resulting from this event. It was the reconciliation of two antagonists, with the sharp demarcation of the boundary-lines to be thenceforth observed by each . . . in reality, the chasm was not bridged over. But if we observe how, under the pressure of this conclusion of peace, the Dionysian power manifested itself, we shall now recognize, in the Dionysian orgies of the Greeks, as compared with the Babylonian Sacaea and their retrogression of man to the tiger and the ape, the significance of festivals of world-redemption and days of transfiguration. Not till then does nature attain her artistic jubilee; not till then does the rupture of the *principium individuationis* become an artistic phenomenon.

The dramatic crisis, towards which the play moves, is related to the action of Barbara Undershaft, granddaughter of the Earl of Stevenage, daughter of a millionaire capitalist, leaving the established church of the established social order to join the Salvation Army. The inheritance of power (the "destructive arms") is kept in the family through the resolution and audacity of her fiancé, who makes his pact with "Dionysos Undershaft," though asserting still: "I repudiate your sentiments. I abhor your nature. I defy you in every possible way." The "transfiguration" which ensues has its appropriate setting in the Garden City of Perivale St Andrews, blueprint for the millennium of social welfare, and its individual enactment in Barbara's change of mood: "She has gone right up into the skies," says Cusins.

Proleptically, the new festivals are represented in the play before Cusins's decisive gesture is made. He himself is ritually prepared for the crisis by an evening spent with Undershaft (shown in the film version, alluded to in the stage play): "he only provided the wine. I think it was Dionysos who made me drunk"; by implication, the drunkenness was spiritual and inspirational, not crudely orgiastic. And the values the dramatist associates with the Salvation Army are multiple, the morality of the soup kitchen, which Nietzsche—Undershaft rejects, being only tangential to it. The spirit of the Salvation Army, as it has attracted Barbara Undershaft, is itself Dionysiac and revolutionary; but it is an enlightened and purified version of older, cruder enthusiasms, which the Hellenistic mind is already able to approve and associate with from the start of the play; for Cusins too, though in pursuit of Barbara, has joined the Salvation Army. In his apologia to Undershaft, he declares:

> I am a sincere Salvationist. You do not understand the Salvation Army. It is the army of joy, of love, of courage: it has banished the fear and remorse and despair of the old hell-ridden evangelical sects: it marches to fight the devil with trumpet and drum, with music and dancing, with banner and palm, as becomes a sally from heaven by its happy garrison. It picks the waster out of the public house and makes a man of him: it finds a worm wriggling in a back kitchen, and lo! a woman. . . . It takes the poor professor of Greek, the most artificial and self-suppressed of human creatures, from his meal of roots, and lets loose the rhapsodist in him.

In fact the reconciliation of Dionysus and Apollo enacted dramatically in act 3 is, in non-dramatic form, imaged from the first, already achieved. Music itself is the sublimation of Dionysiac energy. (The full title of Nietzsche's famous essay is, of course, *The Birth of Tragedy from the Spirit of Music*.)

Shaw actually stages the beginning of one triumphal procession and accompanies it with a shadow-play of the supersession of one religion by another. The form in which the climax, in act 2, is presented may be related to another extract from *The Birth of Tragedy*:

Schopenhauer has described to us the stupendous *awe* which seizes upon man, when of a sudden he is at a loss to account for the cognitive forms of a phenomenon, in that the principle of reason, in some one of its manifestations, seems to admit of an exception. Add to this awe the blissful ecstasy which rises from the innermost depths of man, ay, of nature, at this same collapse of the *principium individuationis*, and we shall gain an insight into the being of the *Dionysian*, which is brought within closest ken perhaps by the analogy of *drunkenness*. It is either under the influence of the narcotic draught, of which the hymns of all primitive men and peoples tell us, or by the powerful approach of spring penetrating all nature with joy, that those Dionysian emotions awake, in the augmentation of which the subjective vanishes to complete self-forgetfulness. So also in the German Middle Ages singing and dancing crowds, ever increasing in number, were borne from place to place under this same Dionysian power. In these St John's and St Vitus's dancers we again perceive the Bacchic choruses of the Greeks, with their previous history in Asia Minor, as far back as Babylon and the orgiastic Sacaea. There are some, who, from lack of experience or obtuseness, will turn away from such phenomena as "folk-diseases" with a smile of contempt or pity prompted by the consciousness of their own health: of course, the poor wretches do not divine what a cadaverous-looking and ghastly aspect this very "health" of theirs presents when the glowing life of the Dionysian revellers rushes past them.

With his presentation of the Salvation Army as a recrudescence of Dionysiac fervour, Shaw extended Nietzsche's medieval analogues to the bacchic chorus into modern times. The image suggested in the last lines of Nietzsche's paragraph may have provided the hint for the episode in which Barbara, who has just witnessed the triumph of Undershaft at which her faith, as it seems, has crumbled, remains a still figure amid the animated scene as the Salvation Army band, caught up in the exultation with Undershaft, marches off with music to the great meeting:

> CUSINS [*returning impetuously from the shelter with a flag and a trombone, and coming between Mrs Baines and Undershaft*]:
> You shall carry the flag down the first street, Mrs

Baines [*he gives her the flag*]. Mr Undershaft is a
gifted trombonist: he shall intone an Olympian diapason to the West Ham Salvation March. [*Aside to
Undershaft, as he forces the trombone on him.*] Blow,
Machiavelli, blow. . . . It is a wedding chorus from one
of Donizetti's operas; but we have converted it . . .
"For thee immense rejoicing—immenso giubilo—immenso
giubilo." [*With drum obbligato.*] Rum tum ti tum tum,
tum tum ti ta—

BARBARA: Dolly: you are breaking my heart.

CUSINS: What is a broken heart more or less here? Dionysos
Undershaft has descended. I am possessed. . . . Off we
go. Play up, there! Immenso giubilo. [*He gives the
time with his drum; and the band strikes up the march, which
becomes more distant as the procession moves briskly away.*]

MRS BAINES: I must go, dear. Youre overworked: you will
be all right tomorrow. We'll never lose you. Now
Jenny: step out with the old flag. Blood and Fire! [*She
marches out through the gate with her flag.*]

JENNY: Glory Hallelujah! [*flourishing her tambourine and
marching*].

UNDERSHAFT [*to Cusins, as he marches out past him easing the
slide of his trombone*]: "My ducats and my daughter"!

CUSINS: [*following him out*]: Money and gunpowder!

BARBARA: Drunkenness and Murder! My God: why hast
thou forsaken me?
*She sinks on the form with her face buried in her hands. The
march passes away into silence.*

The exclamatory dialogue contributes to the excitement; the syntax of
logical speech has little place here. The crescendo of sound is intensi-
fied by the gathering in of themes, the drawing together of the various
symbolic perspectives in which Shaw presents his fable during the
course of the play. Cannon and thunder, elemental and divine, as well
as the strong pulse of life, are to be heard in the beating drum. But the
sense of emotional and mental violence communicated at this point
comes chiefly from the harshly ironic intersection of moods: exhilaration set against agony. Horror at the contemplation of destructive
power is transformed through identification with that power; pity is
rejected for recognition of agony as a further inverted celebration of

violent energy. Shaw had perhaps remembered that comedy and tragedy alike have been traced back to the satyr chorus of the Dionysiac
festival. There is no doubt that audiences are infected by the exhilaration. The conventional reaction to the sentimental appeal of a deserted
heroine is pressed into service to give a keener edge to Cusins's brutal
denial of sympathy and emphatic reassertion of unmixed joy. We
should like to recoil from him, but cannot. The experience is a bril-
liantly conceived vehicle for the loss of self-possession in a transport of
irrational feeling. Shaw is demonstrating something very like a physical law: the superior power of volume of sound, weight of numbers,
releasing energy under the pressure of an intensifying rhythm. And the
march remains a wedding march as the gentle-mannered Cusins confronts the chagrin of a subdued Barbara with a bridegroom's self-
regarding exultation.

Yet the impression of the single figure in its stillness persists: there
is strength of another kind in this maintained integrity and isolation. It
is the apollonian will in Barbara that holds out now. And with the
shock of recognizing in her final cry, "My God: why hast thou
forsaken me?" the words of the Christian divine saviour, the audience
is returned to thoughtfulness.

"There are mystical powers above and behind the three of us,"
declares Undershaft in the screen version. The shadows of Dionysus
and Apollo are to be glimpsed shiftingly behind Undershaft himself,
Cusins and Barbara, but Barbara alone is the Christ figure of the play:
its action represents her ministry, her betrayal and abandonment by
her disciples, and her agony; leaving off the uniform of the Army is a
kind of death; visiting the munitions factory of Undershaft and Lazarus,
she harrows hell. The multiple symbolism of the play's final setting
suggests, as Shaw chooses to bring the various implications dramatically to life, Golgotha, in the dummy corpses of mutilated soldiers; the
exceeding high mountain of the Temptation; the mount of the Ascen-
sion, with a view of the New Jerusalem itself, where Peter Shirley has
been given the job of gatekeeper and timekeeper.

Shaw, indeed, introduced a valid criticism of Nietzsche when he
identified the Salvation Army not only with the worshippers of
Dionysus, but also with the Church Militant of the risen Christ. His
representation of Christianity as a variety of dionysiac religion corrects
Nietzsche's exaggeration of its "subjective" quality, which made possible his over-schematic view of the opposition between Christianity
and Dionysus—Antichrist. The preface to *Major Barbara* distinguishes

between true Christianity and Crosstianity, the religion of negation, of sin and guilt, suffering and death, submission and deprivation. Within the play, a process of redemption is enacted through a bargaining for souls and a vicarious sacrifice. It is a redemption of Christianity itself. Undershaft does not destroy the Salvation Army; he is ready partly to identify himself with it, more ready to identify it with himself, as, in order to win Barbara, he buys it with his cheque to Mrs Baines, the Commissioner. Barbara's spiritual pilgrimage takes her through disillusion and despair to a rebirth of hope and a new vision. Her private emotional experience enforces the recognition that "the way of life lies through the factory of death," that destruction has its proper place in a healthy scheme of things, and even religion and morality must change in order to survive. Her spiritual death and resurrection contain the promise of a new social order: the money for which she was betrayed bought the freedom of Bill Walker's soul. What this freedom implies is given rational definition in Cusins's declaration of his own new-found purpose:

> I now want to give the common man weapons against the intellectual man. I love the common people. I want to arm them against the lawyers, the doctors, the priests, the literary men, the professors, the artists, and the politicians, who, once in authority, are more disastrous and tyrannical than all the fools, rascals and impostors. I want a power simple enough for common men to use, yet strong enough to force the intellectual oligarchy to use its genius for the general good.

The purging of obsolete and unworthy elements in Barbara's Christian faith is accompanied by revision of its liturgy. This process begins in act 1, when the household, except for Stephen, is seduced from family prayers to the more original and vital form of service conducted by Barbara in the drawing room. It opens to the strains of *"Onward, Christian Soldiers, on the concertina, with tambourine accompaniment."* The emblematic sword, which Undershaft has referred to as the sign of his works, is already at least as appropriate as the cross in the insignia of Barbara's religion; and Shaw certainly expected his audience to supply the remembrance of Christ's words, "I came not to send peace but a sword." Cusins's excuse to Lady Britomart is unserious in manner and may easily be taken as simple camouflage; but rejecting, as it does, the terms of the General Confession, it at least calls into question the common sense of perfectionism and the morality of self-abasement and excessive emphasis on guilt:

> you would have to say before all the servants that we have done things we ought not to have done, and left undone things we ought to have done, and that there is no health in us. I cannot bear to hear you doing yourself such an injustice, and Barbara such an injustice. As for myself, I flatly deny it: I have done my best.

Undershaft later proposes a revision in the Church Catechism to admit that "Money and gunpowder" are the "two things necessary to Salvation." His account of the works of mercy follows from an identification of the deadly sins with the burdensome material necessities of "Food, clothing, firing, rent, taxes, respectability and children." Stephen, in act 1, supplies the address of the Undershaft business as "Christendom and Judea." This serves as a warning note of a half-hidden movement in the play from the Old Testament (and ancient Greek) morality of just exchange to the New Testament morality of forgiveness and love. In effect, these are reconciled through the rejection of false and facile interpretations of the New Testament admonitions. Cusins's point of agreement with Undershaft, "forgiveness is a beggar's refuge. I am with you there: we must pay our debts," is the necessary counterpoise to that repudiation of irrational guilt in act 1 (quoted above). Cunningly Undershaft confounds his daughter in answering her charge, "Father do you love nobody?" by carrying the meaning of love to the extreme of "Love your enemies":

> UNDERSHAFT: I love my best friend.
> LADY BRITOMART: And who is that, pray?
> UNDERSHAFT: My bravest enemy. That is the man who keeps me up to the mark.

Cusins's admiring response to this, "You know, the creature is really a sort of poet in his way," does more than acknowledge the Socratic unfolding of neglected truth in a paradox; it conveys a recognition of beauty in the healthy ambivalence of strong emotions, an admission very necessary in the lover of Barbara that aggression need not be ugly and mean. His repudiation of beggarly forgiveness prepares for her new version of the Lord's Prayer:

> I have got rid of the bribe of bread. I have got rid of the bribe of heaven. Let God's will be done for its own sake: the

work he had to create us to do because it cannot be done except by living men and women. When I die, let him be in my debt, not I in his; and let me forgive him as becomes a woman of my rank.

This is so different from conventional humility, it could unkindly be termed arrogance and found unattractive. For the most part, Shaw manages to endear us to a heroine whose actual living counterpart might well repel us. He does so by suffusing the portrait with his own warm appreciation of the type and setting it off by contrast with a minor sketch of a more conventionally admirable woman.

Orthodox Christianity has a truer representative in Jenny Hill, the Salvation Army lass, than in Barbara Undershaft, and Jenny's Christian spirit is a sublimation of her womanly nature. Jenny is the natural victim of the bullying male; turning the other cheek in response to Bill Walker's assault, offering forgiveness instead of revenge and treating her suffering as matter for joy. She merits her place in the triumphal band, bearing her tambourine, for she has positive qualities that Shaw admires: genuine courage and cheerfulness and industry in the cause she has at heart; this is a credible instance of the "worm . . . in the back kitchen" become a woman, a daughter of the Highest. But Jenny's morale (she is only eighteen) is fed by her admiration of Barbara, and there are weaknesses in her that lessen her appeal. Her conventional expressions of piety often strike a false note; her insistence on *love* is too facile; her pity is equally sentimental. Neatly, Shaw demonstrates something unpleasant in her excessive sympathy; Barbara's sense of the ridiculous, like Undershaft's antagonisms, conveys a truer respect for human dignity, for the independence and privacy of the soul:

> BILL [*with sour mirthless humour*]: Aw was sivin anather menn's knees at the tawm. E was kneelin on moy ed, e was. . . . E was pryin for me: pryin camfortable wiv me as a cawpet. Sow was Mog. Sao was the aol bloomin meetin. Mog she says "Aw Lawd brike is stabborn sperrit; bat down urt is dear art." Thet was wot she said. "Downt urt is dear art!" An er blowk thirteen stun four!—kneelin wiv all is wight on me. Fanny, ain't it?
>
> JENNY: Oh no. We're so sorry, Mr Walker.
>
> BARBARA [*enjoying it frankly*]: Nonsense! of course it's funny. . . .

JENNY: I'm so sorry, Mr Walker.

BILL [*fiercely*]: Downt you gow being sorry for me: youve no call. . . . Aw downt want to be forgive be you, or be ennybody.

If Shaw was concerned to attack the morbid sentimentality of late Victorian Christianity, he was—he needed to be—ready likewise to attack the womanly ideal associated with it. The imbalance between Jenny's emotional and intellectual development has made her the dupe of society, unawake to realities, assisting the millionaire's daughter in collecting the pennies of the indigent in her tambourine, as the wealthy good-for-nothing Lomax takes them in his hat. There is an analogy to be drawn between her and Barbara, who, with the same power of work and need to expend herself in a cause, has to be cured of a similar blindness to things as they are, saved from an equal frittering away of her quality in a cause unliberated from a capitalist economy. Certainly G. B. S. does not repudiate wholesale the Christianity that Barbara and Jenny share; it is its vulnerability and self-betrayal that he rejects. So, in the symbolic structure of his play, he has replaced Christ by the Female Warrior, an androgynous type presiding over the new religion. In the setting aside of the old interpretation of woman's role, along with other forms of masochism, an ideal of sexual equality is implied.

The whole play is flagrantly concerned with money. The first scene, set in the luxurious and stately library of the house in Wilton Crescent and dominated by the opulent physical presence of Lady Britomart, laps us round in an atmosphere of womblike security. The unreality of material need and adversity, in this context, comes through all the more clearly for Lady Britomart's talk of economy. If it were anxious talk, the whole effect would be destroyed; but there is no anxiety in Lady Britomart's make-up: she is the abundant and never-failing earth-mother of the peak of the golden year. In explaining to Stephen their financial situation, she is merely eliciting the moral approval she thinks due to her; she knows the easy and comfortable solution to her problems—such as they are!—and will apply it quite unscrupulously and without false pride; for she is free of the personal uncertainty that needs to worry about pride. In the first few minutes of the dialogue, we learn of the money available: the Lomax millions (though Charles will not inherit for ten years); the "poverty" of the Earl of Stevenage on "barely seven thousand a year" and her own personal income, enough to keep one family in its present luxury. The date is 1906, and the value of the pound is high. Anyway, Shaw has thoughtfully provided a cost-of-living index within the play: thirty-eight shillings a week is the standard wage paid by that model employer, Andrew Undershaft; in the first scene itself, her mother's standard of "poverty" can be measured against the reference to Barbara discharging her maid and living on a pound a week—a gesture with more of eccentricity about it than real asceticism, for she still lives in Wilton Crescent and, when we see her, is the perfect representative of physical well-being—plump with nourishment, rosy-cheeked and "jolly" with health, brisk with energy. The immediate prospect is, perhaps, a little more serious for Sarah Undershaft and Charles Lomax, "poor as church mice" on £800 a year, as they are less richly endowed by nature. But there is always the comforting thought of the unseen providence who has only to be supplicated: the absent father, "rolling in money," "fabulously wealthy." Not a hint of the uncertainties of great wealth creeps into the dialogue, no shadow of sudden losses and bankruptcies, only of the chances of picking up a fortune. In every generation since the reign of James I some foundling has succeeded to the vast Undershaft inheritance; and "they were rich enough to buy land for their own children and leave them well provided for," apart from the main bequest. Through the centuries the wealth has been accumulating without a break, it seems. This play is certainly not haunted by the Malthusian nightmare.

In this respect, its world is that of folklore and fairy tale, of Dick Whittington and Jack and the Beanstalk; a world of inexhaustible hoards of treasure, where straw can be spun into gold and geese lay golden eggs; a world ruled over by luck and indulgent to its favourites: the young, the beautiful, the cheerful, the quick-witted and, not least, the hopeful stranger who carries off the prize from the legitimate heir. The conditions of the will made by Charles Lomax's father establish the genre: "if he increases his income by his own exertions, they may double the increase." They reveal a principle of economic distribution that could be called natural, though it is also familiar in Christian terms: "To him that hath shall be given"; the proposition is that the naturally endowed are fittest to control the resources of civilized society. *Major Barbara,* in its unfolding, extends the principle beyond economic bounds: power to the strong; authority to the commanding.

The fictional situations on which Shaw's plays turn are often absurd and fantastic. Their remoteness from credible actuality works curiously in alliance with the excessively rational element. The arbitrariness of the fable, as an excuse for the play, is flaunted: Shaw is not dramatizing a story with a moral, but creating a dramatic image of his conflicting emotions and ideas. The blatant casuistry with which Cusins matches the doubtful relevance of the test—claimants for the Undershaft inheritance must prove that they are foundlings—communicates the dramatist's sense of logic as a game, his mind's self-delight in its own free play, and a scorn for the plodding literalist. More seriously, it communicates his sense of the slipperiness of all attempts to interpret life rationally. Casuistry is a common element in fairy tales. But the foundling motif is not without serious significance. In relation to Shaw's own psyche, the foundling figure is here interestingly linked with the images of providential bounty and the blueprint for a benevolent paternalism.

The conversion of Barbara, on which the play turns, is essentially conversion to the acceptance of wealth. As part of Shaw's campaign against idealism, or more precisely "Impossibilism" as it was currently termed among the Fabians, *Major Barbara* sets itself against false pride in unrealizable commodities. Beyond the temptation to refuse tainted money lies the more pernicious temptation to keep out of the marketplace altogether. The position from which Cusins has begun to emerge in pursuit of Barbara, when the play begins, represents the negation from which he and Barbara have to be saved: the retirement of the intellectual, poet, or saint, possible only as a form of privilege (Oxford—surely it is Oxford?—being in 1906 no more an exposed position in society, no less comfortable than Wilton Crescent, as Lady Britomart's acceptance of Cusins recognizes; scholars are gentlemen, and "nobody can say a word against Greek"). Shaw uses Cusins's intellectual clarity to make explicit, near the end of the play, the realist's view of selling the soul in compromise with the world:

> It is not the sale of my soul that troubles me: I have sold it too often to care about that. I have sold it for a professorship. I have sold it for an income. I have sold it to escape being imprisoned for refusing to pay taxes for hangmen's ropes and unjust wars and things that I abhor.

Before we reach this point, our acceptance of the statement as a truism has been prepared by Shaw's confrontation of the Faustian theme of the bargain with its connotations in the central Christian myth.

Undershaft as Mephistopheles, *Doppelgänger* to Cusins's Faust, is presented as a sham villain in a sham conflict. He is more like Cusins than at first appears probable, the stage "heavy," but intellectualized, no more dionysiac in temperament and character than Cusins, the self-confessed apollonian. The two together provide the play with twin foci of ironic consciousness, mutually comprehending; Undershaft merely reveals to Cusins what he already knows, in order to elicit admission of the knowledge: intellectually they are from the start equally free of illusions. They watch each other's manœuvring for the winning—or betrayal—of Barbara; they may talk of rivalry, but the total view they present is more like complicity.

It is in act 2, where Undershaft and Cusins observe the working out of the subplot, or inset play, involving Barbara and Bill Walker, that Shaw concentrates awareness of the Christian analogues: the price received by Judas for the betrayal of Christ and the sanctified bargain of the Redemption, the sacrifice which ransoms human souls. The act begins with the frauds, the minor characters of Rummy Mitchens and Snobby Price ("Snobby's a carpenter," says Rummy, so preparing for our recognition of the fullness of Bill Walker's pun: "Wot prawce selvytion nah? Snobby Prawce! Ha! ha!"). Both are unscrupulous in their readiness to benefit from the providence of the Salvation Army. (Rummy and Lady Britomart, it seems, are sisters under their skins.) They epitomize a natural way of regarding wealth, opposed to Peter Shirley's and Bill Walker's legalistic way. Peter talks conscientiously in terms of paying for what he gets and being himself paid a just price for what he gives. Bill, attempting legalistically to buy the natural freedom of his soul, throws his sovereign on the drum, where it is followed by Snobby Price's cap; Snobby, the instinctive, unregenerate socialist, is a parasite on legality, as well as the self-justified petty thief preying on such master-thieves as Undershaft and Bodger. Barbara, alluding to Bill's "twenty pieces of silver" and suggesting that her father need contribute no more than another ten "to buy anybody who's for sale," gives the gesture its ironic ambiguity: in the miniature play, the ostensible object of the bargain is Bill's soul and Barbara is both tempter and cheapjack working up the bidding—"Dont lets get you cheap," as she works up the collection at Army meetings; the greater price paid for Barbara herself, in the cheque handed over to Mrs Baines by Undershaft, cancels out Bill's payment and is the token of his release from his bond; the second payment is not only a magnified reflection of the first, but its sacramental transfiguration.

The folk law, to which the Undershaft tradition adheres, bears a genuine relation to the mythology at the centre of the play and to the ritual of the Dionysiac festivals in which Attic drama is believed to have originated, ritual celebrations of the rebirth of God in a divine foundling. In the present Shavian context, official Christianity is certainly reborn as natural religion after the symbolic "death" of Barbara. (Cf. Prosperpine's descent into the Shades.) But there is also present the suggestion of a foundling Apollo inheriting from Dionysus. The transmutation of this into the fairy-tale of the boy from Australia who takes up the challenge and proves himself worthy of the kingdom and the hand of the princess, that traditionally go together, does much to save *Major Barbara* from pretentiousness. It might limit its power to disturb, if the ironic ambiguity of the end of the play was not realized—a realization important also to the success of the play in performance (for, without the edge such an interpretation gives, act 3, so exciting to read, could well fall dramatically flat after act 2—as it did when the play was first produced at the Court Theatre).

Major Barbara is no exception to the tendency of Shaw's plays to reflect the pantomime form of fairy-tale, or mythological material, while relying on the fundamental unity in such different forms of imaginative construct. Britomart, Barbara and Undershaft are Edwardian incarnations of Demeter, Persephone and Dis/Minos (more easily recognizable as such in the years just following Arthur Evans's first exhibition of finds from the Knossos site than their counterparts in *Candida* had been); but also there is a touch of that sham villain, the demon king, about Undershaft, and in the grouping of Britomart and Barbara an intriguing resemblance to the association of the pantomime Dame with the Principal Boy. In the course of the play, a number of references are made to Barbara's self-evident likeness to her mother. The most broadly comic is assigned to Lady Britomart herself in the opening scene:

> Ever since they made her a major in the Salvation Army she
> has developed a propensity to have her own way and order
> people about which quite cows me sometimes. It's not lady-
> like: I'm sure I dont know where she picked it up.

The whole of this scene is an emphatic demonstration of Lady Britomart's matriarchal domination of her son, Stephen. She accuses him of fiddling first with his "*tie*," then with his "*chain*," and the objects are certainly emblematic of his relations with her. The trick is later repeated in her scene alone with Undershaft:

> LADY BRITOMART: Andrew: you can talk my head off; but you cant change wrong into right. And your tie is all on one side. Put it straight.
> UNDERSHAFT [*disconcerted*]: It wont stay unless it's pinned [*he fumbles at it with childish grimaces*].

Here Andrew takes on the aspect of Jove in a nineteenth-century classical burlesque, bullied by his consort. The parental reconciliation which seems implied in the last act denotes more than the acceptance by society of an unpalatable truth, the reconciliation between power and the "incarnation of morality." When Undershaft has won his daughter, his wife sweeps in to appropriate the empire he has built up. The last glimpse we are given of Barbara represents her clutching "*like a baby at her mother's skirt.*"

In retrospect, the action of the play, initiated by Lady Britomart, can be seen as the working-out of her purpose: to absorb and assimilate the potentially hostile forces, adding them to her own strength. Nations are revitalized in this way; and who else but Britannia at her most imperial have we here? But the persistent victory of the mother over her children, her power always to *contain* them, is more ambiguous in its value. Barbara claims to take a less narrowly domestic and material view than her mother—

> I felt like her when I saw this place—felt that I must have it—that never, never, never could I let it go; only she thought it was the houses and the kitchen ranges and the linen and china, when it was really all the human souls to be saved.

—but she is equally possessive, and her similar tendency to treat men as children implies that the pattern will continue in the next generation. She addresses her fiancé invariably by the pet name of "Dolly" (Lady Britomart, with the formality of her period, calls him reprovingly "Adolphus"); even when he has seemingly passed the test of manhood by accepting Undershaft's challenge, he remains to Barbara "Silly baby Dolly," and she can cry exultantly: "I have my dear little Dolly boy still; and he has found me my place and my work." The child keeps the doll, the mother keeps the child, the Stevenages maintain their ascendancy through the instrumentality of the strangers they annex. The Earl of Stevenage, Lady Britomart claims, suggested the inviting of Andrew to Wilton Crescent. Whether we take this eponymous ancestor of the conventionally philistine Stephen to be a smokescreen or an actual presence in the background, the sense of ulterior motivation remains, and the sense of a consciousness, like the author's, foreseeing and embracing the whole dramatic development. Bill Walker warns Cusins of the fate before him, as he relates his own experience of Barbara to what may be in store for her "bloke":

> Gawd elp im! Gaw-aw-aw-awd elp im! . . . Awve aony ed
> to stend it for a mawnin: e'll ev to stend it for a lawftawm.

Martin Meisel has classified Barbara's wooing of Bill Walker's soul as an example of the reversed love-chase (in which the woman is the pursuer). Certainly it offers a reflection of, or insight into, Cusins's fate. It is in relation to Bill that we chiefly see demonstrated Barbara's capacity for chivvying and bullying, and Shaw leaves us in no doubt of the hidden pressures on her side: her self-confidence is the manner of her class, the product of money, of social prestige and the habit of authority, the certainty of police protection and support. What subdues Bill, before ever Barbara appears to him, is the information that she is an earl's granddaughter; when her millionaire father turns up, he involuntarily touches his cap; the brute force and skill of Todger Fairmile, already won over to Barbara's faith, are her final weapons.

Male vulnerability to the woman's ethic of respect for weakness, shame and guilt is recognizably caricatured in the boastful "Snobby" Price, whose official confession, "how I blasphemed and gambled and wopped my poor old mother," is balanced by his private admission to Rummy, "She used to beat me," and who runs out the back way when his mother arrives at the gate. Bill's blow to Jenny Hill's face is his repudiation of this ethic; making reparation for the act, in preference to being forgiven, is the next stage in his discovery of a morality that does not rob him of his self-respect and self-responsibility. Class distinction no longer cows him when he has paid his debt. Before his exit, near the end of act 2, he is able to take his leave of the desolate Barbara with the magnanimity and good humour of an equal, restored to freedom. He checks his instinctive gesture towards his cap, and he does not take the hand she puts out to him—that would be acceptance of middle-class manners, and Bill can now afford, as he prefers, to keep proudly to his own: "Naow mellice. Sao long, Judy." It is a recognition of an integrity in her that matches his own. Her "Passion," as well as her betrayal by the rest, has thus played its part in saving his soul—from guilt, gloom, slavery and negativism.

Fergusson's critique of *Major Barbara* refers to the Wilton Crescent setting of act 1 as though it was retained throughout the play. His interpretation of it as "the London version of the bourgeois world" 's appearing to Shaw "as stable and secure as the traditional cosmos of the Greeks or Elizabethans," is not simply an affront to Lady Britomart's aristocratic breeding; it disregards the extent to which Shaw has fantasticated the locale through the characters he gathers there and the dialogue they speak, not least by introducing "Salvation" music among the games of the young people. In fact, the play destroys any possible illusion that this is a naturalistic interior and not a richly furnished stage to accommodate the superhuman stature of Lady Britomart and Andrew Undershaft, sprung from the gutter to become secular master of the world. But Fergusson's mistake can be related to the impression other critics have got from the end of the play. Alick West, seeing in it Shaw's capitulation to bourgeois values and decisive desertion of Marxist socialism, ended serious consideration of Shavian drama, in *A Good Man Fallen among Fabians*, at this point. Indeed there are sections of Marcuse's 1966 preface to *Eros and Civilization* on the actualities of our "advanced industrial society" which it is useful to place beside the situation Shaw has brought his characters to, in Perivale St Andrews. Marcuse is concerned with the difficulty, in an affluent society, of breaking "the fatal union of productivity and destruction, liberty and repression" and learning "how to use the social wealth for shaping man's world in accordance with his Life Instincts, in the concerted struggle against the purveyors of Death":

> The very forces which rendered society capable of pacifying the struggle for existence served to repress in the individuals the need for such a liberation. . . . In the affluent society, the authorities are hardly forced to justify their dominion. They deliver the goods; they satisfy the sexual and the aggressive energy of their subjects. Like the unconscious, the destructive power of which they so successfully represent, they are this side of good and evil, and the principle of contradiction has no place in their logic.

Only in the name of Undershaft and perhaps the Wedding Chorus that reminds us that *Major Barbara* is, like *Widowers' Houses*, in part a marriage play, does Shaw take sexual energy into account. Otherwise Marcuse's diagnosis is uncannily close to the terms in which Shaw has resolved the philosophical dilemma of his play. Undershaft has successfully induced Barbara to abandon the principle of contradiction for the faith that "There is no wicked side: life is all one," and the question must be asked, whether she has truly gone *beyond* good and evil, or whether the unity of vision beyond moralistic duality has been achieved at the cost of a vital distinction. Perhaps she and Cusins *have* lost their way and been subtly tricked by the older generation ("The odds are overwhelmingly on the side of the powers that be," Marcuse remarks). The political preface to *Eros and Civilization* takes a historical perspective:

> This situation is certainly not new in history: poverty and exploitation were products of economic freedom; time and again, people were liberated all over the globe by their lords and masters, and their new liberty turned out to be submission, not to the rule of law but to the rule of the law of the others. *What started as subjection, by force soon became "voluntary servitude," collaboration in reproducing a society which made servitude increasingly rewarding and palatable. The reproduction, bigger and better, of the same ways of life came to mean, ever more clearly and consciously, the closing of those other possible ways of life which could do away with the serfs and the masters, with the productivity of repression.* (My italics.)

I do not think Shaw was confused or uncertain, but fully conscious of the perilous ambiguity of the situation. The last line of his text is an alert:

UNDERSHAFT [*to Cusins*]: Six o'clock to-morrow morning,
    Euripides.

And the undercutting of the dramatic resolution in the reduction of Cusins and Barbara in the last moments is functional in referring the problem back to the audience. It implies a recognition (which Brecht later shared) that the true resolution of socialist drama belongs not in the work of art but outside it in society. Cusins's choice is a resolution in terms of plot; as a total structure of ideas the play remains a paradox in which antitheses retain their full value and cannot be resolved away. The many churches in Perivale St Andrews are not only confirmation of the comparative mythology built into the play; they represent rival visions and issues undecided. There is nothing static about this New Jerusalem: snobbery and the sense of hierarchy survive, but they are confronted by the principles of the William Morris Labor Church.

Barbara is aware that the efficient industrial society, however prosperous, is not the fulfilment of her vocation but its opportunity. Her purity of intention, what the nineteenth century called "character" and what *On the Rocks* was to call "conscience," is relied on still to find its way through a perspective of infinitely proliferating ironies. Singleness of purpose is necessary to action; but conversely, Shaw's drama now implies, the purity of the action needs to be safeguarded by a matching skepticism, an understanding of things that has moved beyond the defensive self-irony of *Candida* to become a well-forged weapon of assault against "the purveyors of Death."

The Marriage of Contraries

J. L. Wisenthal

Since Shaw's preface to *Major Barbara* is presented as an explanation of the play, one might begin a discussion of the play by looking at it. The opening section of the preface is entitled "First Aid to Critics," and the next begins by saying that Shaw is driven "to help [his] critics out with Major Barbara by telling them what to say about it." In accepting Shaw's help, however, critics might bear in mind his own critical dictum that "the existence of a discoverable and perfectly definite thesis in a poet's work by no means depends on the completeness of his own intellectual consciousness of it." And what Shaw says about the play in the preface does not, in any case, necessarily represent his whole view of it. His explanations of everything are deliberately one-sided: he brings to his public's attention the aspects of a question which he wishes them to consider.

The aspect of *Major Barbara* which Shaw wished his readers to consider, or which he himself saw as the essence of the play, is the economic one. The second section of the preface is entitled "The Gospel of St Andrew Undershaft," and this gospel has to do with money and poverty—according to the preface. After his statement that he will tell critics what to say about the play, Shaw begins to do so: "In the millionaire Undershaft I have represented a man who has become intellectually and spiritually as well as practically conscious of the irresistible natural truth which we all abhor and repudiate: to wit,

From *The Marriage of Contraries: Bernard Shaw's Middle Plays.* © 1974 by the President and Fellows of Harvard College. Harvard University Press, 1974.

that the greatest of our evils, and the worst of our crimes is poverty, and that our first duty, to which every other consideration should be sacrificed, is not to be poor." In the play itself Undershaft's gospel is twofold. His religion, he tells Cusins in act 2, is "that there are two things necessary to Salvation . . . money and gunpowder." In the preface the second article of Undershaft's faith is not really dealt with at all; the manufacture of weapons is referred to only in an economic context, as the profession which was his alternative to poverty: "Undershaft, the hero of Major Barbara, is simply a man who, having grasped the fact that poverty is a crime, knows that when society offered him the alternative of poverty or a lucrative trade in death and destruction, it offered him, not a choice between opulent villainy and humble virtue, but between energetic enterprise and cowardly infamy." This argument is identical with Shaw's analysis of Mrs. Warren's profession (see preface to *Mrs Warren's Profession*), and Undershaft's gospel, as presented by Shaw in the preface to *Major Barbara*, is no different from Mrs. Warren's in essentials.

In many ways *Major Barbara* is similar to *Mrs Warren's Profession*. According to Archibald Henderson, Shaw told him that "perhaps a more suitable title for this play [*Major Barbara*] . . . would have been *Andrew Undershaft's Profession*," if it had not been for the fact that he had already used the formula twice before, in *Mrs Warren's Profession* and *Cashel Byron's Profession* (the novel that he wrote in 1882). Both *Major Barbara* and *Mrs Warren's Profession* proclaim Shaw's instrumentalist, relativist morality: one must act, not from any absolute moral principles, but according to the practical demands of a particular set of circumstances. Both Undershaft and Mrs. Warren make the more moral choice—that is, the more practical, useful one—while Mrs. Warren's half-sisters and Peter Shirley illustrate the error of basing one's actions on the dictates of conventional "morality." Given a badly organized society which forces one to choose between "moral virtue" and material well-being, it is more moral to be "wicked" than to be good. In both plays a high-minded daughter learns unpleasant truths about the real world through a parent whose profession represents its most shocking features; and each daughter must decide whether to accept or reject her parent. Although Barbara and Vivie make opposite choices, they both base their choice on the desire not to be useless, and they both reject the life of the leisured middle-class lady.

Also, *Major Barbara*, like *Mrs Warren's Profession*, is much concerned in a direct way with money. In the masterly opening scene Lady

Britomart has summoned Stephen to discuss the family's money problem with him; his sisters' impending marriages, she tells him, require
her to find a way of increasing the family's income. It is this necessity
that sets in motion the events of the play: Undershaft, the provider of
money, is brought into contact with his family after a separation of
many years. In this first scene Stephen is disillusioned about the source
of his wealth in a way reminiscent of Vivie's disillusionment by Crofts
(and of Trench's discovery in act 2 of *Widowers' Houses*).

> LADY BRITOMART: I must get the money somehow.
> STEPHEN: We cannot take money from him. I had rather go
>   and live in some cheap place like Bedford Square or
>   even Hampstead than take a farthing of his money.
> LADY BRITOMART: But after all, Stephen, our present income
>   comes from Andrew.
> STEPHEN [*shocked*]: I never knew that.

This nicely anticipates, in a minor and comic way, Barbara's shattering
discovery in act 2 that because she is a member of the Salvation Army
her money "comes from Andrew" and his like. Similarly, Lady
Britomart's statement to Stephen that "it is not a question of taking
money from him or not: it is simply a question of how much"
anticipates the Salvation Army's behavior in act 2 in rejecting Bill
Walker's pound while accepting Undershaft's five thousand. The
question in both cases is not a moral one, but a practical, economic
one. As Frank Gardner says to Praed, in a remark which sums up so
much of *Mrs Warren's Profession*, "It's not the moral aspect of the case:
it's the money aspect." It would be true to say that in *Major Barbara* the
first act is in part concerned with the economic problems of the rich,
the second with the economic problems of the poor, and that in both
cases the money comes from Undershaft. The settings of all three acts
draw one's attention to the importance of money. The Salvation Army
shelter in act 2 is a symbol of the fruits of poverty, while the aristocratic
opulence of Wilton Crescent and the bourgeois amenity of Perivale St.
Andrews reveal the advantages of money. Undershaft himself points
to the contrast between the cannon works and the shelter: "I see no
darkness here, no dreadfulness. In your Salvation shelter I saw poverty,
misery, cold and hunger." Undershaft is here justifying the superiority
of his kind of salvation over that of the Salvation Army, and in the
speeches of his that follow he proclaims the importance of money and
the sinfulness of poverty.

But is the need for money the central concern of *Major Barbara*? In order to answer this, one must ask how important it is that Undershaft's way of making money is the manufacture of weapons. Given what Shaw says in the preface about the play, Undershaft's profession could be anything lucrative and unsavory: he could be a slum landlord like Sartorius, a brothel owner like Crofts, or a distiller like Bodger. But if he had been one of these, the play would have been profoundly different. There is a crucial distinction between Undershaft's profession and the others: weapons can be a direct instrument of social change, which slum dwellings, brothels, and whisky are obviously not. Undershaft defends gunpowder in a way in which the other immoralists could not defend their wares. He does not simply say (as Mrs. Warren does) that it is better to engage in disreputable activities than to starve: he goes much further than Mrs. Warren in that he offers a positive defense of his weapons as the necessary means of reforming society. The climactic debate at the end of the play is more concerned with gunpowder itself as an instrument of change than it is with its manufacture as a source of money. The debate ends with Undershaft's challenge to Cusins, "Dare you make war on war?" and Cusins is more central than Barbara in act 3 as a whole. But Cusins is mentioned only once in the preface, and then only as the "Euripidean republican" who is perfectly understood by Undershaft. The preface is prefatory mostly to act 2 and hardly at all to act 3, for it is in act 3 that the second article of Undershaft's faith is dealt with. The conflict in act 3 is not about money, except in the indirect sense that Barbara is offered well-fed men to save (and note that although they are well-fed, they still need saving: money is a means, not an end). Undershaft talks about the choice that he made as a young man not to be poor, but no party to the debate is in fact poor; neither Barbara nor Cusins joins the cannon works in order to acquire money. The play would have been more consistent with the preface (and of course a much less interesting play) if Peter Shirley's decision to join the cannon works, rather than Cusins's, had formed the basis of the final act. But as the play stands, the preface provides a very misleading introduction to it.

II

Major Barbara is not so much about money as about power. It can best be seen as an exploration of the nature of power: the possession of control or command over others. The word itself occurs twenty-eight times in the last fourteen pages of the play, and all through the play examples are to be found of different kinds of power, of which money is only one. We have seen, for example, that the power of money is made manifest in the scene between Lady Britomart and Stephen. But so is Lady Britomart's power over Stephen: the power of an authoritarian, domineering mother over an uncertain, immature son. In the course of the play she loses her power over Stephen, who is the only person she has really dominated: clearly an authoritarian personality by itself is of little use. Undershaft, who is less authoritarian and domineering than his wife, has more power; and Cusins, who is far less authoritarian than either of them, has in a sense more significant power than anyone else in the play, as we shall see later.

The Bill Walker episode in act 2 dramatizes various kinds of power. Bill's own kind of power is brute force, which is a crude and inadequate version of Undershaft's weapons. The parallel with Undershaft, in fact, extends further: both Bill Walker and Undershaft are trying to win a young woman back from the Salvation Army (and Undershaft has fallen in love with Barbara, "with a father's love"); both have determination and a touch of brutality; and both offer money to the Salvation Army. A stage direction at the end of act 2 describes Bill as *"unashamed,"* which is Undershaft's motto. I think that one of the functions of the Bill Walker episode is to demonstrate these parallels between Bill Walker and Undershaft: parallels which suggest both Bill's potential strength and Undershaft's limitations.

Also related to the major strands of the play is Bill's near-conversion. It is brought about largely by Barbara, but not entirely by her. He is subdued as well by the threat of superior physical force in the person of Todger Fairmile, the wrestler; he speaks with *"undissembled misgiving"* when he learns that it is Todger Fairmile who has taken his girlfriend from him, and his belligerence disappears. As Bill says on the point of conversion, "Aw cawnt stend aht agen music awl wrastlers and awtful tangued women." This almost successful combination of Barbara's religious power and the brute force of Todger Fairmile prefigures the union of Barbara and Undershaft at the climax of the play.

Barbara's power over Bill is itself a mixture of various kinds. The first factor to subdue him has nothing to do with her personal qualities: he is much taken aback when Peter Shirley tells him that "the major here is the Earl o Stevenage's granddaughter"; and his awe of the aristocracy is clearly one of the reasons why Barbara is able to deal with him while Jenny Hill is not. Another factor is Barbara's ladylike self-possession and calm superiority in handling Bill, as opposed to Jenny Hill's lack of self-control. That these qualities of Barbara's can be attributed to her aristocratic background is implied by what Lady Britomart says in act 1: "It is only in the middle classes, Stephen, that people get into a state of dumb helpless horror when they find that there are wicked people in the world. In our class, we have to decide what is to be done with wicked people; and nothing should disturb our self-possession." In this, as in her power to command her subordinates in the Salvation Army, Barbara is her mother's daughter.

But the principal element in her near-success with Bill is what she has inherited from her father: her religious nature. She derives personal forcefulness and the ability to sway others from her feeling that she is working not for her own happiness but for a larger purpose. She feels herself to be an agent of the Life Force, which she calls God. Her religion, though, is not based (at any point in the play) on the two articles of her father's creed, money and gunpowder. Nor is it the traditional Christianity of the Salvation Army. As Cusins tells Undershaft, "Barbara is quite original in her religion." Barbara's religion, which is revealed mainly in her wooing of Bill Walker's soul, has to do with making men of people.

> BARBARA [*softly: wooing his soul*]: It's not me thats getting at you, Bill.
> BILL: Oo else is it?
> BARBARA: Somebody that doesnt intend you to smash women's faces, I suppose. Somebody or something that wants to make a man of you.
> BILL [*blustering*]: Mike a menn o me! Aint Aw a menn? eh? Oo sez Aw'm not a menn?
> BARBARA: Theres a man in you somewhere, I suppose.

In the same scene she urges Bill to "come with us . . . to brave manhood on earth and eternal glory in heaven." By the end of the play Barbara has decided to get "rid of the bribe of heaven," but it does not seem to have played a very significant role in her soul-saving while she was in the Salvation Army. Her desire is not so much to ensure Bill Walker's entry into heaven as to make him behave decently on earth. This is Shaw's own concept of religious conversion, expressed, for example, in Tanner's account of his acquisition of the "moral passion" in the first act of *Man and Superman*, and dramatized in *The Shewing-up of Blanco Posnet* (1909). The really religious people, Shaw wrote to

Janet Achurch in 1895, "have dignity, conviction, sobriety and force"; religion "substitutes a profound dignity and self-respect for the old materialistic self."

Barbara's way of converting Bill Walker to manhood is to make him aware that he is not yet a man: to awaken a sense of sin in him. This is akin to what Shaw considered part of his own role as an artist. "It annoys me to see people comfortable when they ought to be uncomfortable," he says in the Epistle Dedicatory to *Man and Superman*; "and I insist on making them think in order to bring them to conviction of sin." According to Shaw's Lamarckian view of evolution, life can progress only if individuals desire to improve, and it is therefore vital that they be made aware of the need for self-improvement. The giraffe will not make the effort to acquire a longer neck until it feels that its present neck is too short.

This religion of Barbara's is directly contrary to what Shaw regards as a principal element in conventional Christianity: the belief that one can be saved without changing one's behavior—by atonement, forgiveness, punishment, or vicarious redemption. In the section of the preface entitled "Weaknesses of the Salvation Army," Shaw writes that he does not think that "the inexorability of the deed once done should be disguised by any ritual, whether in the confessional or on the scaffold. And here my disagreement with the Salvation Army, and with all propagandists of the Cross (which I loathe as I loathe all gibbets) becomes deep indeed. Forgiveness, absolution, atonement, are figments: punishment is only a pretence of cancelling one crime by another; and you can no more have forgiveness without vindictiveness than you can have a cure without a disease. You will never get a high morality from people who conceive that their misdeeds are revocable and pardonable, or in a society where absolution and expiation are officially provided for us all." It is when Christian redemption is unavailable that the ruffian feels obliged to cease to be a ruffian. Then, as Shaw puts it in the preface to *Androcles and the Lion,* "the drive of evolution, which we call conscience and honor, seizes on [our] slips, and shames us to the dust for being so low in the scale as to be capable of them." The awakened conscience of the thief "will not be easy until he has conquered his will to steal and changed himself into an honest man by developing that divine spark within him which Jesus insisted on as the everyday reality of what the atheist denies." It is this divine spark that Barbara refers to when she says to Bill Walker, "Theres a man in you somewhere, I suppose."

The precise position of the Salvation Army on this key question of redemption is not made plain in the play, and the preface is self-contradictory. After the passage quoted above about Shaw's deepest disagreement with the Salvation Army, Shaw says that Bill "finds the Salvation Army as inexorable as fact itself. It will not punish him: it will not take his money. It will not tolerate a redeemed ruffian: it leaves him no means of salvation except ceasing to be a ruffian." This is the way in which Barbara treats him in the play, but the Salvation Army's policy is left unclear. One does notice, however, that Jenny Hill asks Barbara whether she might take some of the money which Bill offers "for the Army," and that Bill's conversion is frustrated—or at least postponed—when he sees that the Salvation Army accepts the money of Bodger and Undershaft, thus apparently offering them automatic salvation instead of demanding a real moral conversion. Shaw also remarks in the preface that members of the Salvation Army "questioned the verisimilitude of the play, not because Mrs Baines took the money, but because Barbara refused it." The implication of both preface and play is—although neither makes this entirely explicit—that Barbara's religion is, all through the play, different from that of the Salvation Army in that she alone uncompromisingly rejects the conventional Christian concept of salvation.

III

A reading of *Major Barbara* that based itself on the preface might see Undershaft as one of the ideal heroes of Shaw's plays and as Shaw's spokesman in this play. For in the preface he is presented as if he were the *raisonneur* of the play, who demonstrates the inadequacies of the points of view of the other characters, particularly of Barbara. The preface implies that the play is about the justified triumph of Undershaft's gospel over that of Barbara and the Salvation Army. We have seen that Cusins, who is Undershaft's chief opponent in the climactic debate of the final act, is barely mentioned in the preface.

In the play itself, of course, Undershaft is by no means an unattractive character. Part of his attractiveness lies in his power, and it is important to recognize just what is the nature of this power, and what its limitations are. His power is mainly of three different kinds. There is his will to survive, the power that enabled him to say as a young man, "Thou shalt starve ere I starve." There is the religious power which he shares with Barbara—the energy, vitality, and instinctive grip over others that come from the conviction that one is serving a just and irresistible purpose. Then there is the power of weapons, of which he is the manufacturer and symbol, and the power of money, of which he is the possessor. These qualities are, for the most part, what I called in discussing *Man and Superman* [elsewhere] Philistine qualities. There are some elements of the Realist in Undershaft—his argumentative powers, his consciousness of his role, and his desire to change the world (although these last two, as we shall see, are equivocal) —but his leading characteristics are those of the Philistine, of Ann and Violet in *Man and Superman*. The principal differences between Undershaft and Ann and Violet are that he manifests these characteristics in the marketplace rather than the drawing room, and that he is more articulate than they. But while he is more articulate, what he articulates is a point of view very close to theirs. He believes, as Ann does, in the primacy of the acquisitive will. Much of his philosophy is an elaboration of Ann's remark to Octavius that "the only really simple thing is to go straight for what you want and grab it." Like Ann—and like Nietzsche's aristocrats—he is the beast of prey, stopping at nothing to get what he wants. His methods are more direct than those of Ann and Violet, as he is a man of business rather than a lady of leisure, but unscrupulous, predatory instincts dominate the behavior of all three. Buying the Salvation Army is to the marketplace as a chase across Europe or secrecy about one's marriage is to the drawing room.

Like Ann and Violet, Undershaft is able to get his own way: his overpowering of Cusins is directly comparable to Ann's overpowering of Tanner. In both cases there is the suggestion of some instinctive irresistible force. We have seen [elsewhere] the way in which Ann overcomes Tanner, in spite of his desire to escape: she is an incarnation of the Life Force. In *Major Barbara* Undershaft overcomes Cusins not only with arguments but also with a comparable energy, which is called by Cusins Dionysiac (Dionysos being his name for the Life Force). Here is part of the scene between them at the Salvation Army shelter.

> CUSINS: . . . Barbara is quite original in her religion.
> UNDERSHAFT [*triumphantly*]: Aha! Barbara Undershaft would be. Her inspiration comes from within herself.
> CUSINS: How do you suppose it got there?
> UNDERSHAFT [*in towering excitement*]: It is the Undershaft inheritance. I shall hand on my torch to my daughter. She shall make my converts and preach my gospel—

CUSINS: What! Money and gunpowder!

UNDERSHAFT: Yes, money and gunpowder. Freedom and power. Command of life and command of death.

CUSINS [*urbanely: trying to bring him down to earth*]: This is extremely interesting, Mr Undershaft. Of course you know that you are mad.

UNDERSHAFT [*with redoubled force*]: And you?

CUSINS: Oh, mad as a hatter. You are welcome to my secret since I have discovered yours. But I am astonished. Can a madman make cannons?

UNDERSHAFT: Would anyone else than a madman make them? And now [*with surging energy*] question for question. Can a sane man translate Euripides?

CUSINS: No.

UNDERSHAFT [*seizing him by the shoulder*]: Can a sane woman make a man of a waster or a woman of a worm?

CUSINS [reeling before the storm]: Father Colossus— Mammoth Millionaire—

Cusins, who is never entirely overcome by Undershaft, recovers; but at the end of the act he prepares to march off with Undershaft, leaving Barbara behind, with the words "Dionysos Undershaft has descended. I am possessed." J. I. M. Stewart objects to Cusins's behavior here: "At the moment of Barbara's utmost despair he has thrown himself so irresponsibly into an ironic Dionysiac masquerade that we retain very little interest in him." But Cusins is not a fool; he *is* possessed by an irresistible power, as Pentheus is in *The Bacchae*. That this was Shaw's intention in these scenes is shown not only in the text, but also in his instructions to Louis Calvert, who created the role of Undershaft at the Court Theatre in 1905. Undershaft's speech to Mrs. Baines near the end of the act about the destructiveness of his weapons is, he says, "sort of a fantasia played on the nerves of . . . [Cusins] and Barbara by Machiavelli-Mephistopheles. All that is needed to produce the effect is steady concentration, magnetic intensity." In another letter Shaw points out to Calvert that once Undershaft decides that Cusins is the man he is looking for, he "takes the lead in the conversation and dominates Cusins at once. It all goes on in a steady progression of force." This letter also tells Calvert how to play the last part of act 3: "And now for the main point, on which the fate of the play depends. If you once weaken or soften after 'Come, come, my daughter: don't make too much of your little tinpot tragedy,' we are all lost. Undershaft must go over everybody like Niagara from that moment. There must be no sparing of Barbara—no quarter for any one. His energy must be proof against everybody and everything. . . . You must sweep everything before you until Lady B. knocks you off your perch for a moment; and even then you come up buoyant the next moment with your conundrum. . . . Conviction and courage: that is what he must be full of, and there is no room for anything smaller or prettier." Shaw sees Undershaft less as a debater than as a man of magnetic intensity and overwhelming energy which captivates Cusins as Ann captivates Tanner.

Like Ann and Violet, too, Undershaft represents the forces of the real world. Money is common to both plays as a symbol of the actual, physical, and immediate. The parallel in *Major Barbara* to sex, which Ann represents, is Undershaft's gunpowder. Just as sex is (along with money) the basic reality of the private, drawing room life which is the *milieu* of *Man and Superman*, so gunpowder (along with money) is the basic reality of the public, political life which is the *milieu* of *Major Barbara*. Undershaft may be a religious figure in that he possesses the Dionysiac energy I have been discussing, but this energy, like Ann's, is devoted to the immediate and the practical.

Undershaft, although he has a much stronger grasp of the world than Barbara or Cusins, is less highly evolved than either of them. His religious vision does not extend as far as Barbara's, and his political vision does not extend as far as Cusins's. In both cases, his vision does not extend to the spiritual; it does not go beyond money and gunpowder.

Like Barbara, he talks about saving souls, but what he means by this is not what Barbara means. Undershaft claims that he has saved the souls of his employees, as he has saved Barbara's soul, by giving his men adequate food, clothing, and shelter. He evidently feels that a man is saved if he has been saved from poverty. He cannot see the need for further evolution beyond material well-being, as Barbara can. Although he describes the lives of his employees with ironic detachment, he does not appear to be dissatisfied with the level of civilization that they have attained: "I dont say, mind you, that there is no ordering about and snubbing and even bullying. The men snub the boys and order them about; the carmen snub the sweepers; the artisans snub the unskilled laborers; the foremen drive and bully both the laborers and artisans; the assistant engineers find fault with the foremen; the chief engineers drop on the assistants; the departmental managers worry the chiefs; and the clerks have tall hats and hymnbooks and keep up the social tone by refusing to associate on equal terms with anybody. The result is a colossal profit, which comes to me." This society is very far from Shaw's ideal. In his essay "The Impossibilities of Anarchism" (1891), for example, he says that in our present, capitalist society snobbery flourishes at all levels except among the very poor. "The moment you rise into the higher atmosphere of a pound a week [wages at the Undershaft foundry begin at thirty shillings], you find that envy, ostentation, tedious and insincere ceremony, love of petty titles, precedences and dignities, and all the detestable fruits of inequality of condition, flourish as rankly among those who lose as among those who gain by it." Undershaft is evidently not disturbed by the "detestable fruits of inequality of condition"; because his employees are not poor, he feels that they are saved.

Barbara's view—and Shaw's view—is that Undershaft has provided not salvation, but the necessary precondition of salvation. Barbara will build on the foundations which her father has provided, and try to convert the men to something beyond Philistine, bourgeois, snobbish individualism. What attracts Barbara to the cannon works are "all the human souls to be saved: not weak souls in starved bodies, sobbing with gratitude for a scrap of bread and treacle, but fullfed, quarrelsome, snobbish, uppish creatures, all standing on their little rights and dignities, and thinking that my father ought to be greatly obliged to them for making so much money for him—and so he ought. That is where salvation is really wanted." An early draft of this speech makes Barbara's concept of her new role more explicit: "I want to begin where hunger and cold and misery leave off. Anybody can convert a starving man: I want to convert prosperous ones. And I will. These souls here shall have the sulkiness and the quarrelling and the uppishness taken out of them by Major Barbara. She will teach them to live with one another, I promise you." What satisfies Undershaft clearly does not satisfy Barbara. In fact, she implies not only in act 1 but also near the end of the play, after she has heard his gospel, that he himself is in need of salvation. When Lady Britomart orders her children to come home with her because Undershaft is "wickeder than ever," Barbara replies, "It's no use running away from wicked people, mamma . . . It does not save them." Undershaft apparently does not feel in need of salvation; he seems to feel no need to develop beyond his Nietzschean individualism, with its self-seeking and its contempt for the common people ("the common mob of slaves and idolaters").

Precisely what Barbara would want Undershaft and his employees to become is not stated explicitly in the play—Shaw, as usual, is concerned more with direction than with goal—but what the play does make clear is that Undershaft's concept of salvation represents only a step on the way to salvation.

His political vision, which is closely related to his religious views, is similarly limited. His society of "saved" men, as we have seen, is a society of individualists: men who have no concept of the community as an organic whole with common goals. His own political philosophy is one of extreme individualism. He is proud of the fact that he never gives his employees orders, that the community at Perivale St. Andrews is self-regulating, without any need for external compulsion. His remedy for poverty is for individual poor men to decide to cease to be poor—to act on their own, as he has done, in demanding money from society. If every man behaved as I did, he claims (and Shaw argues in the preface), then poverty would disappear: "*I* was an east ender. I moralized and starved until one day I swore that I would be a full-fed free man at all costs; that nothing should stop me except a bullet, neither reason nor morals nor the lives of other men. I said 'Thou shalt starve ere I starve'; and with that word I became free and great. I was a dangerous man until I had my will: now I am a useful, beneficent, kindly person. That is the history of most self-made millionaires, I fancy. When it is the history of every Englishman we shall have an England worth living in." It may be true that a nation of Andrew Undershafts would be superior to a nation of Peter Shirleys, but is there much point in urging every man to act as Undershaft has acted? Undershaft is a rare type: he has the enormous force of will to determine not to be poor. In *The Intelligent Woman's Guide to Socialism*, Shaw writes that "in great social questions we are dealing with the abilities of ordinary citizens: that is, the abilities we can depend on everyone except invalids and idiots possessing, and not with what one man or woman in ten thousand can do." And in *Major Barbara* Undershaft himself propounds an environmentalist view of society: economic factors determine human conduct. Poverty is in all ways debilitating; it "strikes dead the very souls of all who come within sight, sound, or smell of it." Undershaft's individualist argument that the solution to the problem of poverty is for the poor to determine, as he has done, not to be poor, is confuted by his own statements on the effects of poverty, which are illustrated in the scene in the Salvation Army shelter. It is also confuted by his own practice: he does not preach to the poor to act as he has done, but gives them jobs with adequate pay. The only person within the play who ceases to be poor is Peter Shirley, and this is not because he has declared "Thou shalt starve ere I starve," but because Undershaft's foundry has employed him. And the foundry can employ only a small proportion of the nation's working class: it is not a real solution to the problem of poverty. The play shows both the best and the worst effects of capitalism, and clearly implies that the blighted lives of the unfortunates at the Salvation Army shelter are more representative than those of the comfortable residents of Undershaft's garden city.

Undershaft, then, has achieved neither the religious nor the political goals of the play. He has not saved souls, in Barbara's and Shaw's sense, and he has not abolished poverty. Nor has he put an end to war. The Armorer's Faith—"to give arms to all men who offer an honest price for them, without respect of persons or principles"—has caused him to provide only the means for the waging of war, not the means for its abolition. His weapons serve no higher purpose of his own, but the lower purposes of "the most rascally part of society," as Cusins points out. Undershaft seems to be quite unaware of these limitations, and yet he is drawn to Barbara and Cusins, who may be able to accomplish what he has not accomplished. His attitude toward them is contradictory: some of his speeches suggest that he sees them as followers, who will carry on his work for him. But in other speeches he challenges them to do work which is profoundly different from his own, and which would entail the overthrow of himself, his foundry, his class, and his gospel.

He tells Cusins in act 2 that Barbara will be his follower, that she will give up her religion for his:

> UNDERSHAFT: . . . I shall hand on my torch to my daughter.
>   She shall make my converts and preach my gospel—
> CUSINS: What! Money and gunpowder!
> UNDERSHAFT: Yes, money and gunpowder. Freedom and
>   power. Command of life and command of death.

In act 3 he continues to talk as if Barbara must give up her religion and practice his. He says, as we have seen, that he has saved the souls of his men; if this is the case, then there is no place for Barbara's religion at the cannon works. But on the following page he issues his challenge to Barbara: not to give up her religion for his, but to preach her own gospel to his employees. "Try your hand on *my* men," he says; "their souls are hungry because their bodies are full." The change now is to be not from one religion to another but from the hungry to the well-fed, in line with Shaw's view that material well-being must precede spiritual improvement. Yet Undershaft is contemptuous of Barbara's concept of salvation:

CUSINS: I . . . want to avoid being a rascal.

UNDERSHAFT [*with biting contempt*]: You lust for personal righteousness, for self-approval, for what you call a good conscience, for what Barbara calls salvation, for what I call patronizing people who are not so lucky as yourself.

Undershaft, then, invites Barbara to convert his men to a religion that he appears to reject, a religion that could supplant his own.

His challenge to Cusins contains a similar contradiction. It is not clear whether he intends him to carry on precisely as he himself has done, or to bring about a new era at the cannon works. The particular question is whether Cusins will remain true to the Armorer's Faith: whether he will sell weapons to anyone who can pay for them, or whether he will provide them only to those who will use them for the benefit of mankind. Undershaft insists that Cusins "must keep the true faith of an Armorer, or you dont come in here." But then on the next page he says to him: "If you good people prefer preaching and shirking to buying my weapons and fighting the rascals, dont blame me." That Undershaft is inviting Cusins to gain control of the weapons in order to fight the rascals is clear from his final challenge to him, "Dare you make war on war? Here are the means." Now, one cannot both sell weapons only to those who can pay for them and at the same time make war on war. If you are loyal to the Armorer's Faith, then you continue to sell arms to the ruling classes—that is, to those who now have them anyway—and society does not change significantly.

These contradictions can be partly accounted for by the fact that Undershaft, a master of irony, is unscrupulously and cleverly appealing to Barbara and Cusins on their own terms. "It is through religion alone that we can win Barbara," he tells Cusins in the scene in act 2 in which he declares that she will preach his gospel of money and gunpowder. Similarly, it is only through high-minded political goals that he can win Cusins. And so he invites Barbara to save the souls of his men and challenges Cusins to make war on war, confident that once they have joined the foundry they will succumb to the spirit of the place and continue as he has done.

But the contradictions are not entirely explained in this way. For they are connected not only with Undershaft's conscious irony, but with contradictions within his own mind of which he is not conscious. His hatred of poverty is genuine. "I hate poverty and slavery worse than any other crimes whatsoever," he says. "And let me tell you this. Poverty and slavery have stood up for centuries to your sermons and leading articles: they will not stand up to my machine guns. Dont preach at them: dont reason with them. Kill them." This is not ironic but impassioned; Undershaft sounds here like a serious revolutionary, and soon after this he is saying to Cusins, "Come and make explosives with me. Whatever can blow men up can blow society up."

Undershaft considers himself bound by the Armorer's Faith, as he considers himself bound by the firm's Antonine tradition of inheritance. He and his six predecessors have all been true to the Armorer's Faith, with the result that poverty and slavery have stood up not only to the sermons and leading articles written by people like Barbara and Cusins but to the seven generations of Andrew Undershafts. What is needed now—and Undershaft seems unconsciously to recognize this—is a new Andrew Undershaft who will reject the Armorer's Faith and sell arms only to those who will use them to fight against war, poverty, and slavery. The play implies that at some level he knows that he himself is inadequate for the task of creating a better society: that powers very different from his own are required as well. In act 2, in his first Dionysiac conversation with Cusins, he proposes an alliance between himself, Cusins, and Barbara: "I am a millionaire; you are a poet; Barbara is a savior of souls. What have we three to do with the common mob of slaves and idolaters? . . . We three must stand to-gether above the common people: how else can we help their children to climb up beside us?" The implication here, whether Undershaft consciously intends it or not, is that the three of them together might be able to do what he alone cannot do. And there are other hints in the play that Undershaft has some sense of his limitations. He tells Lady Britomart that the cannon works "does not belong to me. I belong to it"; and he admits to Cusins that he has no power of his own. Even more significant is his challenge to Barbara and Cusins, which follows Cusins's statement that Undershaft has no power: "If you good people prefer preaching and shirking to buying my weapons and fighting the rascals, dont blame me. I can make cannons: I cannot make courage and conviction." In this speech he is saying in effect that he must rely on "good people" like Barbara and Cusins to reform society, that he cannot do it alone.

Undershaft shows an awareness of the value of dialectical conflict in his desire for strong opponents. He tells Barbara near the end of the play that he loves only his "bravest enemy. That is the man who keeps me up to the mark." When Mrs. Baines mentions that in 1886 the poor broke the windows of clubs in Pall Mall, Undershaft replies, *"gleaming with approval of their method,"* that this forced the rich to contribute to the relief of poverty.

He also tells Mrs. Baines that he is giving money to the Salvation Army "to help you to hasten my own commercial ruin." "It is your work to preach peace on earth and goodwill to men. . . . Every convert you make is a vote against war." He is, of course, being ironic; his purpose in giving the money is to win Barbara from the Salvation Army. But there is a double irony here. By bringing Barbara and Cusins into his cannon works, he *is* hastening his ruin, in that he is handing over the works to people whose values are profoundly different from those on which the foundry rests. And this is what, at his deepest level, he may wish to do.

Undershaft's position is like that of Wotan in Wagner's *Ring of the Nibelung*. Wotan, bound by his treaty with Fafnir, is unable to accomplish his own goal, the retrieval of the ring from him, just as Undershaft, bound by the Armorer's Faith, is unable to fight poverty. Wotan's desire for a hero who will not be bound by the god's treaty and will be able to carry out the deed which he himself cannot is comparable to Undershaft's desire for Cusins to succeed him at the foundry. The relevance of this parallel between Wotan and Undershaft is made clear by the way in which Shaw discusses *The Ring* in *The Perfect Wagnerite*. Before he begins his analysis of *The Valkyries* he tells his readers that "above all, we must understand—for it is the key to much that we are to see—that the god, since his desire is toward a higher and fuller life, must long in his inmost soul for the advent of that greater power whose first work, though this he does not see as yet, must be his own undoing." Wotan, Shaw says earlier, looks for a higher race which will "deliver the world and himself from his limited powers and disgraceful bargains." "On every side he is shackled and bound, dependent on the laws of Fricka and on the lies of Loki, forced to traffic with dwarfs [the instinctive, predatory, lustful, greedy people] for handicraft and with giants [the patient, toiling, stupid, respectful, money-worshipping people] for strength." This reminds one of Cusins's statement, which Undershaft does not really deny, that Undershaft is driven by the cannon works, which in turn is driven "by the most rascally part of society, the money hunters, the pleasure hunters, the military promotion hunters." Undershaft's reply, which is the invitation to Cusins and Barbara to use his weapons to "fight the rascals," is comparable to Wotan's hope that a hero will defy those who limit his power.

IV

In selecting Cusins as his successor, Undershaft is in a sense putting into practice his view that his best friend is his bravest enemy; he chooses his opposite—his anti-self. Cusins is humane, hates war, loves the common people, refuses to accept the Armorer's Faith, and—contrary to the Undershaft tradition—is middle class, of respectable background, and highly educated. According to Shaw, Undershaft decides on Cusins's merit in act 2, just before the first Dionysiac scene. Shaw wrote to Calvert, "The change comes from the line 'And now to business.' Up to that, Undershaft has been studying Cusins and letting him talk. But the shake-hands means that he has made up his mind that Cusins is the man to understand him; and he therefore takes the lead in the conversation and dominates Cusins at once." What has presumably impressed Undershaft is not that Cusins has agreed with any of his views (which he hasn't) but that Cusins has declared, in reply to Undershaft's implied objections to him as a suitor for Barbara, that nothing will stop him from marrying her. And just before the handshake, Cusins responds to Undershaft's "You are a young man after my own heart" with "Mr Undershaft: you are, as far as I am able to gather, a most infernal old rascal." This is the way in which Cusins refers to Undershaft for the rest of the play, and while he is incapable of defending his own point of view against Undershaft's energy and arguments, he insists until the end of the play that he loathes Undershaft's principles. In reply to G. K. Chesterton's statement (in his book on Shaw) that Cusins puts up an "incredibly weak fight" against Undershaft's arguments, Shaw wrote, "As to the professor making no fight, he stands up to Undershaft all through so subtly and effectually that Undershaft takes him into partnership at the end of the play."

The most important difference between Cusins and Undershaft is the difference between the kind of power that each possesses and represents. Undershaft's power, as we have seen, is in the main akin to that of Ann and Violet in *Man and Superman*. Cusins's power is like that of Tanner and Don Juan: the power of imagination and intellect. Shaw's usual view of professors of Greek was not very favorable, but Cusins is based on Gilbert Murray, a close friend whom Shaw admired and respected. He says in the play's prefatory note on Murray that his "English version of The Bacchae came into our dramatic literature with all the impulsive power of an original work," and in *Major Barbara* itself Cusins is presented as a poet, an artist, a thinker (which the true Shavian artist always is). Like all of Shaw's Realists, he has a desire to improve the world around him. As a teacher of Greek he has tried to do this in Tanner's way, through thought, through spirit. He says in the play that his purpose in teaching Greek was to "make spiritual power," and this is amplified in an earlier draft, with the addition to Cusins's speech of the statement that "I am no mere grammarian: if I had not believed that our highest faculties would kindle and aspire at the touch of Greek poetry and Greek thought, I should never have wasted an hour in a class room." In the final version of the play Shaw let the audience infer Cusins's sense of high purpose as a teacher of Greek from the sentence about "spiritual power" and from Cusins's character as a whole.

Cusins's interest is not confined to the university classroom. He tells Undershaft in act 2 that his attachment to the Salvation Army is genuine, in the sense that the Salvation Army inspires people with joy, love, and courage: "It picks the waster out of the public house and makes a man of him: it finds a worm wriggling in a back kitchen, and lo! a woman!" And he objects to Undershaft's contemptuous dismissal of "the common mob of slaves and idolaters." "Take care!" he replies. "Barbara is in love with the common people. So am I." This love of the common people is a characteristic which Cusins shares with his original. Gilbert Murray wrote of himself that as Professor of Greek at Glasgow he tried to combine "an enthusiasm for poetry and Greek scholarship with an almost equal enthusiasm for radical politics and social reform." But he found that the two causes did not always go well together. "Throughout history it has been hard to combine the principles of culture and of democracy, the claims of the few who maintain and raise the highest moral and intellectual standards with those of the masses who rightly do not want to be oppressed." Whereas Gilbert Murray felt that he was able to reconcile these two principles, Cusins is forced to choose one or the other. He chooses the claims of "the masses who rightly do not want to be oppressed"; he decides that it is better to give weapons to the many than civilization to the few. It is not that civilization is necessarily useless, but that it can affect only a minority, while the mass of society is left in the condition of the unfortunates in the Salvation Army shelter. "The world can never be really touched by a dead language and a dead civilization. The people must have power; and the people cannot have Greek." The only kind of power that can be of use to the majority is not the higher power of the spirit but the primitive, physical power of gunpowder. "As a teacher of Greek I gave the intellectual man weapons against the common man. I now want to give the common man weapons against the intellectual man. I love the common people. I want to arm them against the lawyers, the doctors, the priests, the literary men, the professors, the artists, and the politicians, who, once in authority, are more disastrous and tyrannical than all the fools, rascals, and impostors. I want a power simple enough for common men to use, yet strong enough to force the intellectual oligarchy to use its genius for the general good."

In the language of *The Quintessence of Ibsenism*, Cusins, the Realist, wants to provide the common people with Philistine power to use against the Idealists—an idea which is prefigured in Shaw's preface (1900) to *Three Plays for Puritans*. If "the democratic attitude becomes thoroughly Romanticist," he predicts there, "the country will become unbearable for all realists, Philistine or Platonic. When it comes to that, the brute force of the strong-minded Bismarckian man of action, impatient of humbug, will combine with the subtlety and spiritual energy of the man of thought whom shams cannot illude or interest. That combination will be on one side; and Romanticism will be on the other." The implication in Cusins's speech is that the really dangerous people are not those with no ideas—the money hunters, the pleasure hunters, the military promotion hunters—but those with the wrong ideas. Cusins's speech presents the same pattern that we found in *Man and Superman:* the Realist will use aimless Philistine power for a higher purpose, and the real enemy of progress is the Idealist. Cusins will use gunpowder as Tanner will use sex, although Tanner's role is more passive, and he is largely unconscious of it.

In *Man and Superman* the dangers of Idealism are made to seem much greater in the discussion in the Hell Scene than they are in the presentation of life in the Comedy. Similarly, Cusins's discussion here of the misuse of spiritual power has little basis in the rest of the play. The only significant Idealists in the play are Stephen and Lady Britomart, and neither of them seems to represent much of a threat to society. Stephen, as the aspiring politician, comes closest to Cusins's speech, but Undershaft's statement in the first part of act 3 that "*I* am the government of your country," which is confirmed in the second part of the act when the political man is the only member of the visiting party who praises the cannon works unreservedly, would seem to dispose of the political Idealist as an important factor. What one gathers from the play as a whole is that there is no effective "government of your country," that control is in the hands of those who have no social goals: that society is not guided by any purpose, good or bad, but by the primitive acquisitive instincts of those in whom these instincts are strongest. Both *Man and Superman* and *Major Barbara* tell us about the danger of Idealist illusions but make us feel that Philistine power is much more significant. It is not until *Saint Joan* that Shaw's intellectual fear of Idealism becomes something deeply enough felt to be given dramatic expression in characters like the Inquisitor, Cauchon, and de Stogumber. Cusins's speech, in fact, applies much more directly to *Saint Joan* than to *Major Barbara*. It would seem more to the point to arm the common people against the Inquisitor than against Stephen Undershaft.

In spite of this element of contradiction, Cusins's aims are basically clear enough. He will try to create a society which is run for the benefit of the majority by providing the common people with weapons so that they can insist on such a society. Only the threat of revolution, the play implies, will cause the ruling classes to do something about the state of society. In determining to arm the common people, Cusins is determining to reject the Armorer's Faith: he will provide weapons for that part of the community which without his intervention would never acquire them. When Undershaft first tells him of the Armorer's Faith, which (says Undershaft) he must keep if he is to succeed to the cannon works, he unhesitatingly rejects it: "As to your Armorer's faith, if I take my neck out of the noose of my own morality I am not going to put it into the noose of yours. I shall sell cannons to whom I please and refuse them to whom I please. So there!" Undershaft's reply is that "from the moment when you become Andrew Undershaft, you will never do as you please again." So one is left, as one is in so many of Shaw's plays, with a conflict which will continue after the play ends; Cusins intending to depart from the Armorer's Faith, and struggling against Undershaft, "the place," and presumably the "rascals" for whom the weapons are now produced.

Whether or not he succeeds fully, a vital step has been taken: the man of intellect has united with the physical power of the Philistine world.

As in *Man and Superman*, this is in one sense a defeat for the man of intellect and in another sense a victory. It is a defeat in that the intellectual life is given up for the Philistine life: the teaching of Greek for the manufacture of cannons—as in *Man and Superman* the philosopher's activities are given up for those of the father and husband. But as Tanner's submission to Ann may also be seen as a step toward the control of Ann's kind of power by Tanner, so in *Major Barbara* Cusins submits to the foundry so that he can control it. Despite his agreement with Barbara's comment that he will have no power when he enters the foundry, his next speeches, about arming the common people, indicate that he plans to exercise a power which Undershaft has never had: the power of directing the weapons which are made at the foundry. He will put the power of thought to practical use, and his power, like Tanner's, will increase rather than diminish when it combines with that of the Philistine world.

Neither Cusins's kind of power nor Undershaft's is of much use when it exists alone. Undershaft's view that spiritual power without cannons is impotent ("If you good people prefer preaching and shirking to buying my weapons and fighting the rascals, dont blame me") is balanced by Cusins's view that cannons without spiritual power are impotent. His remark to Undershaft that "*You* have no power" equates the maker of cannons with the cannons themselves; the Armorer's Faith reduces Undershaft to an instrument. "I have more power than you, more will," Cusins claims; that is, at least I have the power of mind which designs, seeks conscious goals, and is not a blind force with no purpose of its own. The mild-mannered professor of Greek has more significant power than the tough millionaire cannon manufacturer. This is the same kind of paradox that one finds in *Candida*, in which Marchbanks turns out to be stronger, more manly, and more religious than Morell. Shaw wrote to Gilbert Murray while he was writing act 3, "I have taken rather special care to make Cusins the reverse in every point of the theatrical strong man. I want him to go on his quality wholly, and not to make the smallest show of physical robustness or brute determination. His selection by Undershaft should be a puzzle to people who believe in the strong-silent-still-waters-run-deep hero of melodrama. The very name Adolphus Cusins is selected to that end."

But although Cusins's kind of power may be more meaningful

than Undershaft's, Cusins has done no more than Undershaft to improve society. Each of them has benefited only a relatively small number of people: Cusins his students, Undershaft his employees. And the improvement they have caused in these people has been only partial: Cusins has improved only men's minds, while Undershaft has improved only men's bodies. Cusins and Undershaft, when acting separately, have achieved little of real significance. Only when the spiritual and the material join together can society be improved. "Society cannot be saved until either the Professors of Greek take to making gunpowder, or else the makers of gunpowder become Professors of Greek."

Even this combination of Cusins and Undershaft is not sufficient, however. Cusins, in taking over the foundry, will try to provide "the people" with weapons and hence money, but this could only bring the population up to the level of the employees at the foundry. He would be using his spiritual power in giving the weapons a purpose, a direction, but in order to do this he is giving up the making of spiritual power. In order for men to be saved as well as fed, Barbara's power is required.

Barbara, like Cusins and Undershaft, has been almost—but not quite—ineffectual when working by herself. She does have an effect on Bill Walker, and the play implies that although her attempt to save his soul is frustrated by Undershaft, she has brought about a real change in him. When Barbara tells Bill that she will replace his pound, he replies, in a suddenly improved voice and accent, that he will not be bought by her. And when in the next act she reproaches Undershaft for taking Bill Walker's soul from her, he convinces her that Bill's soul is not entirely lost:

> UNDERSHAFT: Does my daughter despair so easily? Can you strike a man to the heart and leave no mark on him?
> BARBARA [*her face lighting up*]: Oh, you are right: he can never be lost now: where was my faith?

Bill Walker, however, is quite unlike the others whom Barbara is trying to save at the Salvation Army shelter. He has come to the shelter not to beg bread but to demand his girlfriend. He is not noticeably hungry or poor; and he has been able to save two pounds "agen the frost." In fact, he is not very different from Undershaft's "fullfed, quarrelsome, snobbish, uppish" employees, and it is therefore most significant that Barbara converts him, while she has no effect whatever on the others at the shelter, who have come only to satisfy their bodily hunger.

Neither Barbara nor Cusins, then, can have much effect on society while relying exclusively on spiritual power. They (and all those higher beings who want to improve society, of whom Barbara and Cusins are symbolic) must ally themselves with Undershaft, and the forces that he represents. And Undershaft cannot have much effect on society while he relies exclusively on physical power; he needs Barbara and Cusins as much as they need him. What is required is a marriage of intellectual power, religious power, and physical power. This is the real meaning of the alliance which Undershaft proposes in act 2, although no single character in the play is fully aware of the implications of the synthesis. It is left (as usual in Shaw's plays) for the audience to draw the threads together.

Nothing less than a fusion of all three will achieve the implicit goal of the play: a nation of what Barbara would call the saved—a nation of fully developed men and women. Cusins and Barbara without Undershaft would achieve no significant results: political advance is impossible without weapons and religious advance is impossible without money. Cusins and Undershaft without Barbara would achieve, as we have seen, only a nation of Philistines—an extension of the society at the foundry. Barbara and Undershaft without Cusins would achieve only a minority of the saved. Barbara recognizes this: when Undershaft challenges her to convert his employees, her (unanswered) reply is, "And leave the east end to starve?"

The aspect of this union which the play concentrates on is the decision of the two characters with spiritual power to unite with Undershaft: his need for the two of them is only implied, as Ann's dependence on Tanner is indicated only in the Hell Scene of *Man and Superman*. The counterpart in *Major Barbara* of the Hell Scene is the crucial scene between Barbara and Cusins near the end of the play, for it is here that the importance of the more highly developed person is made apparent. Barbara and Cusins seem at the beginning of this scene to have been utterly defeated by Undershaft; but now both of them declare triumphantly that they have found their new purpose, and their speeches in this scene should make it plain that the victory in *Major Barbara* is not Undershaft's alone, just as the Hell Scene should make it plain that the victory in *Man and Superman* is not Ann's alone. Neither Barbara nor Cusins is really converted to Undershaft's gospel of money and gunpowder. They retain their own goals, but see that money and gunpowder are necessary if these goals are to be attained. They see that the higher can be achieved only through the lower. This is an idea which is found in many forms in *Major Barbara*. "Then the way of life lies through the factory of death?" Cusins asks after Barbara has discovered her new role at the end of the play; and Barbara replies, "Yes, through the raising of hell to heaven and of man to God, through the unveiling of an eternal light in the Valley of The Shadow." Similarly, the way of the spirit lies through the flesh (Barbara will convert the well-fed) and the way of peace lies through the sword (Cusins will "make war on war," using weapons to create a world in which war would presumably disappear). The idea is also made explicit in Cusins's defense to Barbara of Undershaft's weapons.

> BARBARA: Is there no higher power than that [*pointing to the shell*]?
>
> CUSINS: Yes; but that power can destroy the higher powers just as a tiger can destroy a man: therefore Man must master that power first.

This is parallel to Barbara's realization that although there is a higher power than money, men must have money first.

Cusins's analogy between Undershaft's weapons and the tiger calls to mind Blake's treatment of wild, destructive power in the *Songs of Experience*. The imagery of Blake's "The Tyger" is that of the foundry, with particular emphasis on fire ("My sort of fire purifies," says Undershaft in act 1). And Blake's poem evokes the combination of terror and attraction that Shaw intends Undershaft and his weapons to produce in Cusins and in the audience—although Blake can create a much greater sense of terror than Shaw. If we assume that Blake's tyger represents the power necessary to overthrow the fallen world of Experience, then the parallel between the poem and the play becomes closer still. Maurice Bowra, who interprets the poem in this way, says that Blake

> sought some ultimate synthesis in which innocence might be wedded to experience, and goodness to knowledge. . . . The true innocence is not after all that of the *Songs of Innocence*, but something which has gained knowledge from the ugly lessons of experience and found an expanding strength in the unfettered life of the creative soul. . . .
> Blake knows well that such a consummation will not

come simply from good will or pious aspirations and that
the life of the imagination is possible only through passion
and power and energy. That is why he sometimes stresses
the great forces which lie hidden in man and may be terrifying but are none the less necessary if anything worth while
is to happen. . . . The tiger is Blake's symbol for the fierce
forces in the soul which are needed to break the bonds of
experience.

Almost everything which Bowra says here about Blake applies precisely to *Major Barbara*. The tiger, like Undershaft, symbolizes a force
from which "good men" recoil, but without which progress is
impossible.

This same emphasis on the necessity of the terrifying is found in
The Marriage of Heaven and Hell. That "the tygers of wrath are wiser
than the horses of instruction" (Plate 9) is exactly what Cusins discovers in *Major Barbara*. *The Marriage of Heaven and Hell* asserts, like *Major
Barbara*, that both forces are necessary: heavenly controlling power and
hellish violent, destructive power must exist together. And in both
works the heavenly is the conventionally good, while the hellish is the
conventionally evil. *The Marriage of Heaven and Hell* tries to break
down and confuse rigid distinctions between heaven and hell, good
and evil, soul and body. It is not true, says the voice of the Devil, that
"Energy, call'd Evil, is alone from the Body; & that Reason, call'd
Good, is alone from the Soul." The truth is that "Energy is the only
life, and is from the Body; and Reason is the bound or outward
circumference of Energy" (Plate 4). Barbara makes a similar discovery:
"Turning our backs on Bodger and Undershaft is turning our backs on
life. . . . There is no wicked side [of life]: life is all one."

Blake's technique of ironic reversal of heaven and hell is an important element in *Major Barbara*. Undershaft is the representative of hell:
Cusins calls him the Prince of Darkness, a devil, Mephistopheles, a
demon, an infernal old rascal; and says that at the Salvation Army
meeting the "brazen roarings" of his trombone "were like the laughter
of the damned." He calls the foundry "this Works Department of
Hell," and Barbara says before the visit that she has "always thought
of it as a sort of pit where lost creatures with blackened faces stirred up
smoky fires and were driven and tormented by my father." The
foundry, which is the center of hellish activity in the play, turns out to
be heavenly ("It only needs a cathedral to be a heavenly city instead of

a hellish one," Cusins observes); while the center of heavenly activity, the Salvation Army shelter, is truly hellish. Undershaft's hell—his diabolical assertive values, his money, and his gunpowder—is the true road to heaven. "You may be a devil; but God speaks through you sometimes," Barbara says after her father has dispelled her despondency about Bill Walker's soul. This parallels Cusins's exclamation near the end of the play that "the way of life lies through the factory of death."

Blake, it is true, values hellish energy more than Shaw does, but both of them present hell as a state just as necessary as heaven in our imperfect world. The unpleasant or frightening cannot be dismissed as evil; Stephen and Lady Britomart are the equivalent of Blake's "Bibles or sacred codes" (Plate 4)—the representatives of conventional absolute morality, whose position is demolished in both works. The moral of the final act of *Major Barbara*, Shaw wrote to Gilbert Murray, "is drawn by Lomax 'There is a certain amount of tosh about this notion of wickedness.' " Morality in both *Major Barbara* and *The Marriage of Heaven and Hell* is relative to the situation and to the individual: "There is only one true morality for every man; but every man has not the same true morality" (Undershaft in *Major Barbara*); "One Law for the Lion & Ox is Oppression" (*The Marriage of Heaven and Hell*, Plates 22–24). *Major Barbara* asserts the necessity of accepting and combining good and evil, heaven and hell; and the best brief statement of its central idea is the aphorism from *The Marriage of Heaven and Hell*: "Without Contraries is no progression. Attraction and Repulsion, Reason and Energy, Love and Hate, are necessary to Human existence" (Plate 3).

Shaw's Moral Vision

Alfred Turco, Jr.

Preliminary Obstacles

Conceptually Shaw's most ambitious play, *Major Barbara* (1905) is also the one least capable of being understood in isolation from his overall development. This drama poses enormous critical difficulties, nearly all of which concern the central character, Andrew Undershaft. Though in my opinion *Major Barbara* is finally not a successful work, it deserves and will repay the most careful study. Lesser writers might well envy Shaw the distinction of having produced a failure on this level.

There are some initial difficulties that must be cleared away. First, one must understand Shaw's technique of treating the play as a kind of game between himself and his audience; second, one must avoid some common misconstructions concerning the relation between Shaw and purported sources such as Nietzsche's *Beyond Good and Evil*; finally, it is important to see that any *literal* interpretation will be distorted. Misunderstanding in almost every instance comes down to confusion on one of the above points.

Many have felt that *Major Barbara* suffers from its author's propensity to carry paradoxical wit to cynical extremes. Why was it necessary for Shaw to trace the well-being of Undershaft's employees to the manufacture of destructive armaments; would not an automobile factory have done as well? A number of readers have followed Chesterton in interpreting Barbara's "conversion" to her father's views

From *Shaw's Moral Vision: The Self and Salvation.* © 1976 by Cornell University. Cornell University Press, 1976.

as the expression of Shaw's rejection of the religious impulse. But does either of these conclusions really follow? Eager to grant his opposition the strongest possible case, Shaw uses weapons of destruction as an example of material power open to the *most* telling challenge and criticism. If he can make his point stick regarding bombs, it will automatically be true of automobiles—whereas the reverse would not be the case. As for religion, the play says nothing whatever concerning spiritual impulses per se. Barbara is neither a recluse nor an ascetic; as a member of the Salvation Army she has already committed herself to a variety of spiritual life that aims to have an impact upon persons in society. Given this commitment, Shaw argues that the premises Barbara uses to realize it are unsound because she has ignored an important factor. But no conclusion may be made concerning monks, nuns, or other religious; in any case, it would be naive to suggest that the creator of Don Juan, Keegan, and the latter "Ancients" had no sympathy for the contemplative life.

These few instances emphasize the extent to which the reader of *Major Barbara* must constantly take an active role. The play is a battle of wits in which the dramatist and his audience attempt to outmaneuver each other and in the process become increasingly involved in an expanding range of ambiguity that makes it difficult to grasp the meaning hidden (to crib a phrase Shaw used in another connection) at "the center of the intellectual whirlpool" (*Back to Methuselah*). But one need not accept Francis Fergusson's conclusion that the "witty dialectics" are purely theatrical and that Shaw cares nothing for his play's correspondence to truth.

The relation of the play to possible sources provides us with an embarrassment of riches—comparisons with Euripides, Plato, Blake, and Nietzsche (to mention a few) can be illuminating provided we understand that Shaw utilizes these writers exactly insofar as it serves his own purposes. To take one example, there are many parallels between *Major Barbara* and *Beyond Good and Evil*; yet the Shavian ethical position surely cannot be equated with Nietzsche's "transvaluation of values." The famous sequence where Undershaft tries in vain to find Stephen a suitable occupation illustrates the point:

> UNDERSHAFT: . . . Well, come! is there *anything* you know or care for?
> STEPHEN [*rising and looking at him steadily*]: I know the difference between right and wrong.

> UNDERSHAFT [*hugely tickled*]: You don't say so! What! no
> capacity for business, no knowledge of law, no sympa-
> thy with art, no pretension to philosophy; only a simple
> knowledge of the secret that has puzzled all the philoso-
> phers, baffled all the lawyers, muddled all the men of
> business, and ruined most of the artists: the secret of
> right and wrong. Why, man, youre a genius, a master
> of masters, a god! At twentyfour, too!

Though both eloquent and pointed, this was not written by a
Nietzschean, but by a moralist who *does* see the world in terms of
good and evil. The Shavian critique of morality is basically a plea that
we be rather more discriminating (in realizing that poverty is a "crime,"
for example) than people usually are in making ethical judgments. To
point out that the passage is inadequate as an explication of Nietzsche
is hardly a valid criticism of the play. Shaw's ethical dualism is a source
of dramatic strength: it is precisely because he considers Barbara's
aspirations morally higher than Bodger's that the Salvation Army's
dependency upon the resources of a distiller is so fraught with poi-
gnancy. Despite the apparent paradox of a merchant of death being
offered as a positive moral force, a brief examination will reveal that
the ethical perspective of *Major Barbara* is the same as that of *The
Quintessence of Ibsenism,* where Shavian relativism also was equivalent
to a pluralism of means employed within a framework of humane
ends.

According to the *Quintessence,* an "ideal" is an illusion that has
been abstracted into an ethical principle. In opposition to the resulting
system of "morality" predicated upon how things "ought" to be,
Shavian comedy reveals an ironic contrast between this artificially
contrived state and the real world. Thus it comes as no surprise to find
Undershaft chiding Cusins: "Ought! ought! ought! ought! ought! Are
you going to spend your life saying ought, like the rest of our moral-
ists?" His exhortations to his daughter insist only that ethics be con-
crete: "You have made for yourself something that you call a morality
or a religion or what not. It doesnt fit the facts. Well, scrap it. Scrap it
and get one that does." However regrettable the "incarnation of morality" whose conscience is clear and duty done when it has "called
everybody names," the Shavian antithesis is not a conscienceless refusal to make judgments but rather an insistence that things be called
"by their *proper* names" (italics mine). In the second edition of the

Quintessence Shaw had insisted that "conduct must justify itself by its effect upon life and not by its conformity to any rule." The morality of *Major Barbara* is the same. When Bill Walker refuses to give his name to Barbara, she puts him down as "the man who—struck—poor little Jenny Hill—in the mouth": he *is* his action. Undershaft is the personification of the relativist whose belief that "there is only one true morality for every man; but every man has not the same true morality" is only the secular equivalent of Barbara's "Our father . . . fulfils himself in many ways." Indeed, if we can understand that Barbara and Undershaft are really saying the same thing in different fashions, we are less apt to be confused by the outcome of the play.

The third difficulty in understanding the drama concerns the danger of literalism, against which Shaw warned in the last paragraph of his preface: "Major Barbara, is, I hope, both true and inspired; but whoever says that it all happened, and that faith in it and understanding of it consist in believing that it is a record of an actual occurrence, is, to speak according to Scripture, a fool and a liar." But it is not necessary to bring the preface to the rescue of the play, the improbability of whose story itself is emphasized by sudden shifts in the manner of treatment. As Abbott remarks, the first act is high comedy, the second is a piece of low-life realism, and the third is sheer utopian fantasy. This mix of styles has the purpose of preventing the reader from orienting himself to the play on a realistic level, of forcing him instead to distance himself from the entire action and make sense of it in some larger terms.

The latter function is also served by the dialogue:

> UNDERSHAFT: May I ask have you ever saved a maker of cannons?
>
> BARBARA: No. Will you let me try?
>
> UNDERSHAFT: Well, I will make a bargain with you. If I go to see you tomorrow in your Salvation Shelter, will you come the day after to see me in my cannon works?
>
> BARBARA: Take care. It may end in your giving up the cannons for the sake of the Salvation Army.
>
> UNDERSHAFT: Are you sure it will not end in your giving up the Salvation Army for the sake of the cannons?
>
> BARBARA: I will take my chance of that.
>
> UNDERSHAFT: And I will take my chance of the other. [*They shake hands on it.*] Where is your shelter?

> BARBARA: In West Ham. At the sign of the cross. Ask anybody in Canning Town. Where are your works?
> UNDERSHAFT: In Perivale St Andrews. At the sign of the sword. Ask anybody in Europe.

Note here the extreme stylization, deliberately calling attention to the artifice of the dialogue. The formal sequence of balance and antithesis in which the characters echo symmetrically each other's phrases functions to remove the play from the realm of literal reality; the very idea of the exchange of visits (the hinge of the plot) suggests a fantasy world, a kind of "just suppose it were possible" situation only a shade removed from "once upon a time." In this atmosphere, everything must be understood figuratively. For instance, when Cusins, the professor of Greek who joined the Army to worship Barbara, ends by saying that he "wants to give the common man weapons against the intellectual man," one critic takes this as a declaration of an intention to give Undershaft's guns to Rummy Mitchens and Snobby Price (the "common people" who appear in the play) and concludes on that basis that the moral of the work is ridiculous (Woodbridge). But it would make as much sense to take Barbara's objection to Bodger's whiskey as proof that the drama was intended as a temperance tract. One must move beyond guns and Bibles to the symbolic oppositions they represent in this Shavian parable.

THE SHAVIAN HERO

Shaw described *Major Barbara* as the last of a "group of three plays." In the first of them, *Man and Superman,* he had dramatized his conception of a union of the practical and the nobly idealistic. Whether a person is mentally in "heaven" or in "hell" depends on whether he is active or indifferent in relation to the goal of creating the Superman. But this development from the pragmatic posture of the earlier plays could be only temporary because it is articulated in the realm of the dream-vision and collapses with Tanner's return to normal life in society. In *John Bull's Other Island* Shaw attempts to make a direct translation of the vision from the realm of the spirit to that of actuality, only to find that a deep dualism divides the "heaven" of the dream from the "hell" of a world in which the desired synthesis of forces is not possible. In *Major Barbara* Shaw attempts to address the problem raised at the end of the preceding play and determine *why* the synthesis had not been possible. The opposition of divergent forces represented by Ann/Tanner and Broadbent/Keegan here becomes more sharply drawn in the contrast between Barbara and Undershaft, that is, between Christ and cannons. Having thus polarized the conflict between wisdom and power in the most extreme terms possible, Shaw ventures a resolution in this climax of his eschatological trilogy.

Like its forerunners, *Major Barbara* employs a symbolism opposing heaven and hell, salvation and damnation. Here Barbara, the representative of spiritual aspiration, is a member of the "Salvation Army"; Undershaft, the wielder of material power, is "the Prince of Darkness." Barbara goes "right up into the skies"; her father's trombone sounds like "the laughter of the damned." Barbara tells ruffian Bill Walker that he's "going to heaven"; but the nature of Undershaft's occupation suggests to the imbecilic Lomax that "getting into heaven" is not exactly his line. Yet almost immediately an apparent paradox arises: although Undershaft is "infernal," "Mephistopheles," and a "cunning tempter," he is also "Father Undershaft," "St Andrew Undershaft," and "a confirmed mystic." Although his armaments factory is the "Works Department of Hell," it is also a lovely town that "only needs a cathedral to be a heavenly city instead of a hellish one." Indeed, Barbara's expectation that Perivale St. Andrews will be "a sort of pit [full of] lost creatures with blackened faces" would have served more accurately as a description of her own Salvation Army shelter. In *Man and Superman* the inversion of the usual connotations of heaven and hell is initially misleading because Shaw's hell really is a place of damnation and his heaven one of salvation. In *Major Barbara* the paradox is misleading because it is not a paradox—the inversions disguise a dynamic relationship that Shaw believes only our conventional prejudice prevents us from perceiving. Unlike Broadbent, Doyle, and Keegan (who remain essentially static in relation to one another), Barbara, Cusins, and Undershaft participate in an exploratory process of growth.

Andrew Undershaft is the culminating figure in a long line of Shavian heroes (beginning with Sartorius) who see their salvation in terms of survival. As he puts it, "I had rather be a thief than a pauper. I had rather be a murderer than a slave. I dont want to be either; but if you force the alternative on me, then, by Heaven, I'll choose the braver and more moral one." Like Mrs. Warren before him, Undershaft refuses to accept the premises of a ruling class that attempts to rationalize exploitation by using idealistic morality to convince the exploited that their miserable state is blessed. He is the realist who, perceiving the hidden truth that "poverty is a crime," rejects the ethic of self-sacrifice, asserts the validity of his own will, and manufactures cannons with the motto "UNASHAMED." In doing so, he fulfills a family tradition: he is the seventh in a line of Undershafts who, like the Antonines, adopted their successors.

Undershaft combines the practicality of Cashel Byron with the self-conscious articulateness of Jack Tanner. But whereas Tanner only thinks he is a strong man, Undershaft really is a strong man, who does not need to flail about in order to create an impression of importance. Eloquent as he is, the cannon magnate's real strength is not revealed in his long speeches but in his short ones—no man ever got more mileage out of a "No," "Thank you," "Just so," or "I shall be delighted." In verbal sparring, he is the master of devastating brevity:

> CUSINS: Well, I can only say that if you think you will get
> [Barbara] away from the Salvation Army by talking to
> her as you have been talking to me, you dont know
> Barbara.
> UNDERSHAFT: My friend; I never ask for what I can buy.
> CUSINS [*in a white fury*]: Do I understand you to imply that
> you can buy Barbara?
> UNDERSHAFT: No, but I can buy the Salvation Army.

While this character represents the practical sense pushed to a frightening logical extreme, Shaw is not making an atavistic return to earlier heroes in his dramas of survival. If Undershaft seems devilish where his forerunners were shrewd, he will at any rate turn out to be a devil with a difference.

His daughter Barbara, in turn, is a minister with a difference; for like her father, she is a moral realist. Never does she really practice the expiatory religion of the Salvation Army, which encourages people to pretend to terrible sins they never committed in order to emphasize the miracle of being "saved" by Jesus. In this context, it is typical that a ruffian named Bill Walker, after striking Army worker Jenny Hill, should try to "atone" for his act by paying a fine in the form of a donation to the Army and, when this is rejected, by attempting to get himself beaten up by a professional boxer named Todger Fairmile. Barbara's refusal to encourage him in such expiatory rites removes external salvation from Bill at precisely the moment he most wants to be punished. Though her terminology is conventional (she is full of words like soul, devil, and God), no less than her father does Barbara place moral responsibility within the conscience of the individual. As Shaw puts it in the preface, she does not want Bill to pay for his villainy, but to cease being a villain. She wants an internal change based upon Bill's own sense of self-esteem, not an external alteration based on subservience to an abstraction. The ruffian disintegrates under this unusual approach. "Awm as good as her!" he snivels helplessly. And if Bill only believed it, he would be.

Shaw admits in his preface that in real life Barbara might have succeeded in enabling Bill to redeem himself. But the salvation of our suffering Everyman in this Shavian morality play is cut short by the appearance of Goods, in the form of Undershaft's matching gift. Lord Saxmundham, formerly Bodger the whiskey distiller, offers to contribute five thousand pounds to the Army, provided that an equivalent sum be supplied by other donors. Not one to let an opportunity like this pass by, Undershaft proceeds to write a check the Army cannot afford to refuse. Cynically concluding that *his* contribution was rejected because it was too small, Bill now turns on Barbara with the famous taunt: "Wot prawce selvytion nah?" Barbara might be asking herself the same question—unable to accept that what's good for Bill is somehow not good for Bodger, she quits the Army. But she does not immediately see that Undershaft may have acted, not to destroy her aspirations, but to bring home to her consciousness the fact that it is impossible to save Bill while society is organized in the present fashion. The spiritual inertia into which Undershaft has plunged his daughter turns out to be no more irrevocable than the physical "deep sleep" [*The Perfect Wagnerite*; all further references to this text will be abbreviated as *PW*] into which Wotan cast Brynhild at the end of *The Valkyries*. The rest of the play deals with Barbara's creative confrontation of her own disillusionment and her attempt to discover "some truth or other behind all this frightful irony."

Perhaps Barbara would have been less distraught had she been present earlier when Undershaft explained the nature of his "religion" to Cusins.

> UNDERSHAFT: . . . There are two things necessary to salva-
> tion. . . . The two things are . . . money and gunpowder.
> CUSINS: . . . Excuse me: is there any place in your religion
> for honor, justice, truth, love, mercy, and so forth?
> UNDERSHAFT: Yes: they are the graces and luxuries of a
> rich, strong, and safe life.

CUSINS: That is your religion?
UNDERSHAFT: Yes.

Here Undershaft's opening line concerning "two things necessary to salvation" seems very definite indeed. But the dialogue that follows qualifies the idea by suggesting that "money and gunpowder" are not a denial of traditional religious values (honor, truth, love, and so forth) but something that makes adherence to them possible. Without enough money and gunpowder "one cannot afford" virtues; but the possession of money and gunpowder alone will not automatically provide them. The implication of the passage is that material power is a "necessary" but not sufficient cause of salvation in the gospel according to St. Andrew. Playing his "game" masterfully, Shaw tempts the careless reader to mistake his surface strategy for his underlying meaning.

The final act contains a similar interchange between Barbara and her father concerning the "souls" of his workmen:

UNDERSHAFT: I save their souls just as I saved yours.

BARBARA [*revolted*]: *You* saved my soul! What do you mean?

UNDERSHAFT: I fed you and clothed you and housed you. I took care that you should have money enough to live handsomely—more than enough; so that you could be wasteful, careless, generous. That saved your soul from the seven deadly sins.

BARBARA [*bewildered*]: The seven deadly sins!

UNDERSHAFT: Yes, the deadly seven. [*Counting on his fingers*] Food, clothing, firing, rent, taxes, respectability and children. Nothing can lift those seven millstones from Man's neck but money; and the spirit cannot soar until the millstones are lifted. I lifted them from your spirit. I enabled Barbara to become Major Barbara; and I saved her from the crime of poverty. . . . It is cheap work converting starving men with a Bible in one hand and a slice of bread in the other. . . . Try your hand on *my* men: their souls are hungry because their bodies are full.

In response to Barbara's demand to know what he *means* by the apparently outrageous claim to have "saved" her soul, Undershaft explains that his material support rescued her *from* "the seven deadly sins" (the counterparts of Juan's "seven deadly virtues" in *Man and*

Superman). Undershaft's gift of freedom from certain external obstacles has a purely negative function: only Barbara could decide what she had been freed *for*. The point is not, as Chesterton thought, that the religious element is defeated, but that "the spirit cannot soar until the millstones are lifted." Undershaft knows that material sustenance is the precondition—*not* the guarantee—of spiritual aspiration: what would be the point of telling Barbara to try her hand on his workers if he seriously meant his earlier boast, "I save their souls," to mean that he has already secured their salvation in a *positive* sense? His point is rather that the workers' "souls are hungry because their bodies are full" —which can hardly seem an ignoble sentiment to the girl who had said in the previous act, "I cant talk religion to a man with bodily hunger in his eyes."

Thus the play's treatment of the question of the proper use of power is a subtle one. It does not claim that if a person has power he will automatically have wisdom, but rather that if a person does not have power no wisdom he does have will be of any use. Integrity and courage by themselves are not enough: for as Cashel Byron had argued long before, "If you havent executive power as well, your courage will only lead you to stand up to be beaten by men that have both courage and executive power; and what good does that do you?" The moral purity Cusins thirsts for is not feasible; as Barbara tells him, "Turning our backs on Bodger and Undershaft is turning our backs on life." Whoever wishes to separate himself from the "wicked side" of things merely guarantees his own impotence before the Bodgers of the world. The Shavian view holds that *all* money is tainted; those who do not have material sustenance want to get it and those who do have it want to keep it: the resulting struggle of wills is only disguised by conventional idealistic abstractions. Shaw attacks the notion (which he sees as a perversion of Christianity) that humane and intelligent persons are obliged to be nicely passive and self-effacing, thereby assuring the triumph of the very evil they are above confronting. The side of life traditionally considered devilish must be controlled before it can be abolished. The attempt to gain such control has its dangers, of course, but the risks must be taken: "You cannot have power for good without having power for evil."

The explanation of this burgeoning militancy in Shaw's art can be sought in his developing political consciousness in real life. Not that *Major Barbara* marks any overt shift in convictions; the play is in some ways a predictable Shavian document. Trenchant descriptions of the effects of poverty make the point that the enlightened wealthy can have no real interest in perpetuating it; the action itself exposes philanthropy as a ruse enabling the unenlightened wealthy to soothe their consciences in the very act of strengthening their privileged positions. But the tone in which Shaw presents these familiar ideas suggests that his patience with the Fabian policy of watchful waiting is now wearing thin. Just two years earlier, "John Tanner" offered a critique of the price paid for respectability by the Fabians, who had come to be well spoken of "not because the English have the smallest intention of studying or adopting the Fabian policy, but because they believe that the Fabians, by eliminating the element of intimidation from the Socialist agitation, have drawn the teeth of insurgent poverty and saved the existing order from the only method of attack it really fears" (*Man and Superman*; all further references to this text will be abbreviated as *MS*). While the use of a persona enabled Shaw deftly to sidestep the suggestion that these sentiments were his own, the gist of "Tanner's" argument must have struck root in his mind by the time he comes in *Major Barbara* to upbraid the poor for being more often complacent than insurgent. Like the Fabian Society, the Salvation Army opts to pursue its goals by working *through* the existing social system, and thus "draws the teeth" of the very class that might otherwise revolt against the oppression that the Army serves to palliate. Moreover, the Fabian essayist who once urged people to "Vote! Vote!! Vote!!!" and held that "when Democracy fails, there is no antidote for intolerance save the spread of better sense" (*Essays in Fabian Socialism*) now creates a leading character who exults in the claim that the "pious mob fills up ballot papers and imagines it is governing its masters; but the ballot paper that really governs is the paper that has a bullet wrapped up in it." Of course, Undershaft (like Tanner) cannot be taken as identical to Shaw, whose own pronouncements on democracy have not *yet* come to emulate his hero's inflammatory rhetoric. Still, Undershaft's utterances cannot be explained away as a mere standpoint being exploited for theatrical effect; for by the end of the play his exhortations have apparently wrought a significant change in Barbara and Cusins. Indeed, after agreeing to terms with "Machiavelli," the Professor moves to within an inch of advocating the kind of insurrectionary class war that ten years previously Shaw had dismissed as romantic nonsense. But what precisely is the young couple's succession to the leadership of the armaments firm supposed to indicate?

To give audiences a clue for following his play's intricate and baffling turns of meaning, Shaw portrays *Major Barbara*'s various conceptual strands dramatically through the developing interrelationships of the three principal characters, who begin by formally representing an opposition between ideas and gradually come to suggest a dynamism that will unite them. We can begin to sense how this process works by examining an important passage at the climax of the third act:

> UNDERSHAFT: . . . Dont come here lusting for power, young man.
>
> CUSINS: If power were my aim I should not come here for it. You have no power.
>
> UNDERSHAFT: None of my own, certainly.
>
> CUSINS: I have more power than you, more will. You do not drive this place: it drives you. And what drives this place?
>
> UNDERSHAFT [*enigmatically*]: A will of which I am a part.
>
> BARBARA [*startled*]: Father! Do you know what you are saying; or are you laying a snare for my soul?

To the student of Shaw this passage is both crucial and inevitable. As far back as his analysis of Ibsen's *Emperor and Galilean,* we saw Shaw's concern with a synthesis of the individual self and the "world-will." In *Man and Superman* this relation was explained in terms of the operation of the Life Force, which the individual serves but which itself exists only insofar as the human mind creates it. Is Undershaft speaking of himself in terms analogous to those previously applied to Maximus, Wotan, and Don Juan? Undershaft is the slave of a cosmic force—he does not drive the factory, it drives him. Yet he is an active agent, for he is part of the will that drives the place that drives him. Cusins is appropriately baffled, but Barbara's startled reaction suggests she understands quite well what her father has implied. Giving up momentarily on the "morality-mongering" Cusins, Undershaft asks his daughter to tell the Professor "what power really means."

> BARBARA [*hypnotized*]: Before I joined the Salvation Army, I was in my own power; and the consequence was that I never knew what to do with myself. When I joined it, I had not time enough for all the things I had to do.
>
> UNDERSHAFT [*approvingly*]: Just so. And why was that, do you suppose?

> BARBARA: Yesterday I should have said, because I was in the
> power of God. [*She resumes her self-possession, withdraw-
> ing her hands from his with a power equal to his own.*] But
> you came and shewed me that I was in the power of
> Bodger and Undershaft. . . . I was safe with an infinite
> wisdom watching me, an army marching to Salvation
> with me; and in a moment, at the stroke of your pen in
> a cheque book, I stood alone; and the heavens were
> empty.

Barbara has reason to be startled by Undershaft's words, for her own speech corresponds almost diagrammatically to his in its conception of the relation between the individual and the cosmos. Barbara is echoing a point already made by Don Juan: that there is nothing so will-less as the drifting of the willful, and nothing so potent as the service of a force that advances from the efforts of those who realize rather than sacrifice themselves. "God" is created by our doing "the work he had to create us to do because it cannot be done except by living men and women." The result is that paradoxical state in which free will and necessity become merged. This is why Barbara can be "in the power of God," while Cusins can claim she is "original in her religion." This is why Undershaft can admit that he has no power while nonetheless believing that he was a "dangerous man" until he had his will. His factory, a larger force to which he belongs, is the "Undershaft inheritance"; Barbara's inspiration, which comes from "within herself," is also the "Undershaft inheritance." No wonder Barbara fears that a snare is being set for her soul and that her father is diabolically wording his speech in terms he knows will tempt her. For while they have almost identical conceptions of the relation between individual and universal wills, Barbara fears that the self may become synthesized with diabolic as well as divine forces: "Oh, how gladly would I take a better [religion] to my soul! But you offer me a worse one." What is the reconciliation that can bring "infinite wisdom" to the empty heavens in this most difficult of Shaw's dramas of ideas?

It may help to clarify matters here to take up again the analogy between Undershaft and Wotan in *The Perfect Wagnerite*. Just as the god's bargain with Fricka to secure efficiency led him to become hedged by unforeseen "tangles and alliances and compromises" (*PW*), so Undershaft's resort to instruments of destruction to ensure his survival has involved an inevitable narrowing of potential. Undershaft did not *want* to have to choose between being a slave and being a murderer any more than Mrs. Warren wanted to choose between prostitution and poverty. While Shaw insists that these characters have made the right decision under the circumstances, the whole force of his social critique depends on bringing home to the consciences of his audience that such choices are made at great personal cost. For all his ebullience, Undershaft is trapped in his trade: the system by which each of his well-fed workers "keeps the man just below him in his place" is a neat model of a repressive power structure; and the implements manufactured in the factory reinforce the worst tendencies of the very society its owner so eloquently condemns! Thus in some ways Cusins is correct in describing the old man as the slave of "the most rascally part of society, the money hunters, the pleasure hunters, the military promotion hunters." Undershaft's response—"Not necessarily"—is extraordinarily tentative, considering its source; furthermore, it is followed by the surprising intimation that the possibility of the Professor's accusation turning out to be wrong no longer depends upon Undershaft himself, but upon Barbara and Cusins instead. Could he have been more serious than we thought when he asked his daughter, "Have you ever saved a maker of cannons?"

That Undershaft was justified in choosing the cannons does not mean that for Shaw they represent a final good. If he looked at the cannon business as an end, Undershaft would be exactly the kind of big bad capitalist that Marxist critics have thought him. The factory has no moral significance whatever in itself—at one stage of human evolution the command of material power is a vital prerequisite to any further development. That Undershaft cannot personally pursue this development is only natural: even Wotan struck the sword into the stone only to learn that "no weapon from the armory of Godhead can serve the turn of the true Human Hero" (*PW*). Undershaft's hope of not being the "slave" of rascals is entirely dependent (as he proceeds to explain) upon good people not preferring "preaching and shirking to buying my weapons and fighting the rascals." But if his auditors lack the "courage and conviction" to rise to the challenge, then his creed has reached an impasse; at that point he can only say "dont blame me," but he cannot carry the matter further because no one man can embody within himself the entire evolutionary process. Shaw clearly believes that Undershaft must be replaced by something higher; perhaps Undershaft thinks so too. Could it not be with an awareness of being the instrument of that higher force that he persuades Barbara and Cusins to take his own power and use it to supersede him?

Undershaft never states directly that such is his purpose, because his perception of it is more intuitive than intellectual. On the level of explicit formulation, his aims are somewhat different; he wants to pass on his torch to his daughter. She "shall make my converts and preach my gospel." What Undershaft thinks he thinks corresponds to Wotan's belief that *his* daughter, Brynhild, will obey his command to slay Siegmund and thus fulfill his obligations to Fricka. But Wotan discovers that his real will does not correspond to his intentions—secretly he *wants* Brynhild to disobey him. Similarly, though Undershaft may promulgate his armorer's faith to sell cannons to all causes and crimes, he can no more tell Cusins what to do with the cannons than Wotan could tell Siegfried what to do with Nothung. Cusins makes essentially this point in asserting his independence ("I shall sell cannons to whom I please and refuse them to whom I please"); and the millionaire's response ("From the moment when you become Andrew Undershaft, you will never do as you please again") means that the Professor will be in the grip of the Life Force, *not* that he will be under the thumbs of the very "rascals" Undershaft proceeds to urge him to fight. Moreover, Barbara's conviction that it is among the "snobbish, uppish creatures" of Perivale St. Andrews that "salvation is really wanted" indicates that she is not accepting the cannons on her father's terms, either. The fact that the aging entrepreneur adopts as his heirs two persons who he senses will be no slavish disciples suggests that there is more in Undershaft's mind than a logic based on pragmatic self-interest can explain.

It was Maximus the Mystic who first propounded the paradox that the "third empire" would require the death of the self and yet would be " 'self-begotten in the man who wills' " (*The Quintessence of Ibsenism*; all further references to this text will be abbreviated as *QI*). Though Wotan gradually learned that the first task of the Hero would be to "sweep the gods and their ordinances" from his path, Siegfried would never have been conceived had not Godhead begun "secretly to long for the advent of some higher power than itself." Like Wotan, Undershaft can be seen as "finally acquiescing in and working for his own supersession" (*PW*). While the culmination he desires is clearly beyond his own achievement, he is nonetheless the active agent who generates the union of wisdom and power, not as in the dream-vision of Don Juan, but in the real world. Barbara and Cusins must achieve it themselves, free from Undershaft's influence, just as Siegfried must actualize his will "without any illicit prompting from Wotan"; yet it is the chief of the gods and the dealer in destruction who catalyze the change. Undershaft's crucial query, "Dare you make war on war? Here are the means [that is, the cannons]," is that pivotal act in which the assertion of his own will becomes one with the will beyond his own. Critics have attacked the famous question he puts to Cusins since it seems to contradict everything Undershaft has affirmed before. If we grant that he is sincere, Undershaft's action logically makes no sense. Yet the kind of sense an evolutionary leap makes must be perceived in relation, not to the order that already exists, but to the higher one it aspires to create. In terms of the conventional life he has risen above, Undershaft's endeavor is either diabolical (a ploy to entice Cusins to disaster) or self-destructive; in terms of the new life he falls short of, the same endeavor is that self-generated aspiration to a state beyond the self which has been the hallmark of the Shavian hero from the beginning. The question "Dare you make war on war?" marks the instant in which Undershaft creates the force he serves: it corresponds exactly to those moments when Don Juan determines to enter heaven, when Wotan hails the coming of the Hero whom he had sought to destroy, when Julian (had he possessed the courage and insight) would have embraced Christ.

The nature of the process Undershaft stimulates and undergoes can be seen in microcosm in the series of "Maxims" which the first six Andrew Undershafts wrote up in their shops. Each of the even-numbered maxims offers an unmitigated pragmatism without refer-ence to values. Number two, for instance, "All have the right to fight: none have the right to judge," amounts to saying "might makes right." On the other hand, maxims one, three, and five connect the philosophy of power to an ultimate goal: God, heaven, and peace respectively (such as "To Man the weapon: to Heaven and victory"). The history of the Undershafts has witnessed an oscillation between blunt pragmatism and an attempt to suggest a possible relation be-tween such pragmatism and some moral purpose. But the final maxim, number seven—"UNASHAMED"— is ambiguous. It could simply be a curt dismissal of objections often raised against the pragmatic orien-tation and would therefore be classified with the even-numbered group. It could also be taken as the end result of all the others thus far—as if after those swings of the pendulum that Satan saw as part of an infinite comedy of illusion (*MS*), the ground has at last been cleared for a change that will radically alter the opposition by transcending it. The seventh maxim is, significantly, that of the present Andrew Undershaft. He is not the culmination of the synthesis, but the instrument that makes it possible. To paraphrase Barbara: he may be the devil, but God speaks through him sometimes.

When Undershaft originally proposed the exchange of visits, Barbara cautioned that the experiment might end in his "giving up the cannons for the sake of the Salvation Army." He replied in turn that it might end in Barbara's "giving up the Salvation Army for the sake of the cannons." Readers have of course taken Undershaft's prediction as a signal of what will later come true, but it would be fairer to note that both prophecies are fulfilled. Barbara and Cusins "give up" the Salvation Army by accepting the cannon factory, and Undershaft gives up his cannons by placing the power they represent at the service of the religious impulse. "Giving up" here means what "succumbing" meant when Maximus explained to Julian: " 'Does not the child succumb in the youth and the youth in the man: yet neither child nor youth perishes' " (*QI*). The respective "professions" of Barbara and Undershaft will now develop in meaningful relation to each other instead of in isolation. If Shaw did not entitle the play "Andrew Undershaft's Profession," it was because the work involved more than Major Barbara's "conversion."

In *Emperor and Galilean,* Maximus lamented that " 'the empire of the flesh [pagan sensualism] is fallen a prey to the empire of the spirit [Christian asceticism]' " (*QI*). At the end of the second act of *Major Barbara,* this situation has been reversed: the empire of the spirit (Barbara's work for the Salvation Army) has fallen prey to the empire of the flesh (Undershaft's weapons as symbols of materialism). The final act of the drama attempts to depict the possibility of a creative merging of forces. Nothing is relinquished: Cusins will take over the "death and devastation factory," into which, however, he brings "capital" of his own ("the subtlest thought, the loftiest poetry yet attained by humanity"). If we see Shaw attempting here to go beyond the dilemma with which *John Bull's Other Island* concluded by returning to re-examine the ideas he had developed in writing about *Emperor and Galilean* and *The Ring,* then the precise function of the role of Andrew Undershaft becomes clear. Maximus's impulse toward " 'the third empire, in which the twin-natured shall reign' " (*QI*) becomes the paradigm for later Shavian patterns of salvation. In each of these works Shaw employs a trinity of characters to illustrate the allegorical scheme

(Julian–Maximus–Christ; Brynhild–Wotan–Siegfried; Broadbent–Doyle–Keegan; Barbara–Undershaft–Cusins). Where the work deals with a (tragic) separation of forces, the first member of the triad (Julian, Broadbent) manifests an opacity that leads to a visionary second member's (Maximus, Doyle) entrapment in what remains a permanent opposition between the first and third. Where the work outlines a (comic) fusion of forces, however, as in *The Perfect Wagnerite* and *Major Barbara,* an initial opposition between the first and second characters (Brynhild–Wotan, Barbara–Undershaft) is transcended by a pivotal act of the second that produces a synthesis-figure (Siegfried, Cusins) in whom all antinomies are to be reconciled. Looking at several works at once, one could say, broadly speaking, that Undershaft is to Broadbent as Wotan is to Julian. The "damned" characters, Broadbent and Julian, mistake the unfamiliar element of the synthesis as a "rival will" which they must overcome; the "saved" characters, Undershaft and Wotan, are heroic because they have the grace to work *with* the process instead of fighting it. The "truth and heroism" that finally overthrow Wotan turn out to be "children of his inmost heart" (*PW*); so the couple who succeed to the Undershaft inheritance are likewise *his* children—the one his real daughter, the other the son he adopts as his spiritual heir. The result is that Undershaft goes under without being overcome; he is reborn as the spirit represented by Cusins, who becomes Andrew Undershaft VIII.

The resemblance of the temperament of Undershaft to that of Wotan is more than an analogue. In a chapter added to *The Perfect Wagnerite* shortly after *Major Barbara* was written, Shaw attempted to explain more clearly why Siegfried, the great synthesis-figure, had disappointed expectations:

> The dominant sort of modern employer is not to be displaced and dismissed so lightly as Alberic in The Ring. Wotan is hardly less dependent on him than Fafnir: the War-Lord visits his works, acclaims them in stirring speeches, and imprisons his enemies; whilst Loki does his political jobs in Parliament, making wars and commercial treaties for him at command. And he owns and controls a new god, called The Press, which manufactures public opinion on his side, and organizes the persecution and suppression of Siegfried.
>
> *The end cannot come until Siegfried learns Alberic's trade and*

shoulders Alberic's burden. Not having as yet done so, he is
still completely mastered by Alberic.

(PW; italics mine)

In Shaw's view, Wagner had paid too little attention to the power
represented by Alberic. A prospect mentioned in passing in the late
nineteenth-century essay (that the greedy dwarf might get the ring
back and "out-Valhalla Valhalla, if not buy it over as a going concern")
had become an early twentieth-century fact. The description of Alberic's
control bears a striking similarity to Undershaft's address to Stephen
when the latter accuses his father of insulting the government of his
country:

> The government of your country! *I* am the government of
> your country: I, and Lazarus. Do you suppose that you and
> half a dozen amateurs like you, sitting in a row in that
> foolish gabble shop, can govern Undershaft and Lazarus?
> No, my friend: you will do what pays us. You will make
> war when it suits us, and keep peace when it doesnt. You
> will find out that trade requires certain measures when we
> have decided on those measures. When I want anything to
> keep my dividends up, you will discover that my want is a
> national need. When other people want something to keep
> my dividends down, you will call out the police and mili-
> tary. And in return you shall have the support and applause
> of my newspapers, and the delight of imagining that you are
> a great statesman.

The point-by-point resemblance between the two speeches is less remarkable than the relevance to *Major Barbara* of the concluding idea in
the addition to the *Wagnerite*. "Siegfried shouldering Alberic's burden"
comes as close as four words can to describing what Undershaft
attempts to bring about in this play. The dream of the union of
wisdom and efficiency cannot be realized unless the Hero controls the
forces of evil. Undershaft is determined that Cusins shall learn the
lesson that "Alberic's work . . . is necessary work," and that to be
above doing it is to be annihilated by it: the power of the shell "can
destroy the higher powers just as a tiger can destroy a man: therefore
Man must master that power first." Far from being a glorification of
material power, this is a warning against its dangers.

The connection between *The Ring* and *Major Barbara* can hardly be coincidental. In *The Rhine Gold,* Alberic's smithy "resounds with the clinking anvils of the dwarfs toiling miserably to heap up treasure for their master" (*PW*); Undershaft's works, where employees are (in Barbara's words) "all standing on their little rights and dignities" is the equivalent force under a more enlightened directing intelligence. Siegfried does not know who his parents are and laughs at the pedantries of Mime; the Undershaft tradition holds that the business must be left to a foundling who has no education. *Siegfried* is the third of a group of operas just as *Major Barbara* is (according to Shaw himself) the third of a group of plays. *The Rhine Gold,* the first part of *The Ring,* ends with a vision of perfection in the mind of Wotan; *Man and Superman,* the first work in Shaw's eschatological trilogy, supplies an equivalent "great thought" in the vision of Don Juan. In *The Valkyries* Wotan's attempt to implement his vision leads to complications that conclude in a deadlock in which the god, on a hill of fire, "with a breaking heart, takes leave of Brynhild"; *John Bull's Other Island,* an attempt to explore the implementation of Juan's ideal in a real world, ends with the principal characters (on a hillside during sunset) pitifully divided from each other. *Siegfried* depicts, through the instrumentality of Wotan, the triumph of Siegfried, a "perfectly naive hero" (*PW*), in a universe from which Alberic has conveniently disappeared; *Major Barbara* depicts, through the instrumentality of Undershaft, the ascendancy of Cusins, an intellectual of the humanist tradition, in a universe determined to master Alberic. Having analyzed the causes of Siegfried's political failure, the dramatist attempts to provide a modern equivalent who will succeed and enable the race to achieve salvation. *Major Barbara* is Shaw's attempt to rewrite *Siegfried* in terms valid for the twentieth century.

THE BRIDGE AND THE ABYSS

Criticisms of *Major Barbara* fall into three main categories. The first and most influential is Eric Bentley's conclusion that the synthesis represented by Cusins occurred to Shaw too late to be integrated into the rest of the play; the second is the objection that Shaw's treatment of Undershaft is overly clever and intellectually incoherent; the third is the common charge (somewhat related to the first) that the ending is unsuccessful. The first two of these issues can be answered convincingly; that the last cannot be suggests the key to the play's failure.

At what point did the idea of synthesis occur to Shaw? When

Lady Britomart announces in the first scene that Andrew Undershaft is going to pay the family a visit, Barbara is the only person who is not disturbed by the prospect. After the invited but not very welcome guest arrives, Lady Brit's embarrassment about Barbara's work for the Salvation Army provokes a significant interchange:

> LADY BRITOMART: It is not my doing, Andrew. Barbara is old enough to take her own way. She has no father to advise her.
>
> BARBARA: Oh yes she has. There are no orphans in the Salvation Army.
>
> UNDERSHAFT: Your father there has a great many children and plenty of experience, eh?
>
> BARBARA [*looking at him with quick interest and nodding*]: Just so. How did *you* come to understand that? . . .
>
> UNDERSHAFT: . . . I am rather interested in the Salvation Army. Its motto might be my own: Blood and Fire.
>
> LOMAX [*shocked*]: But not your sort of blood and fire, you know.
>
> UNDERSHAFT: My sort of blood cleanses: my sort of fire purifies.
>
> BARBARA: So do ours. Come down tomorrow to my shelter— the West Ham shelter—and see what we're doing.

The conflict is not, as we should expect, between Barbara and her father; Barbara *and* Undershaft are aligned against Lady Brit and Lomax. Barbara is surprised at the understanding from an unexpected quarter, and she can hardly be displeased that her father is not ready to concede that the Army's blood and fire is not "his sort." When Lady Brit rebukes Barbara for talking as if religion were a pleasant subject, Undershaft replies that he does not find it an unpleasant one; on the contrary, "it is the only one that capable people really care for." In addition, both father and daughter agree that the human race cannot be divided neatly into good men and scoundrels. The conventional associations attached to their respective "professions" makes Undershaft and Barbara *seem* to be in opposition when their outlooks are essentially similar. Barbara senses this only vaguely, remarking in the next act to Peter Shirley: "You wouldnt think he was my father, would you?" But readers are entitled to reply: yes, we would.

The same unlooked-for interrelatedness can be discovered between Undershaft and Cusins, beginning with their first meeting:

LADY BRITOMART: This is Stephen.

UNDERSHAFT: Happy to make your acquaintance, Mr Stephen. Then [*going to Cusins*] *you* must be my son. [*Taking Cusins' hands in his*] How are you, my young friend? [*To Lady Britomart*] He is very like you, my love.

CUSINS: You flatter me, Mr Undershaft. My name is Cusins: engaged to Barbara. [*Very explicitly*] That is Major Barbara Undershaft, of the Salvation Army. That is Sarah, your second daughter. This is Stephen Undershaft, your son.

UNDERSHAFT: My dear Stephen, I beg your pardon . . . Mr Cusins: I am much indebted to you for explaining so precisely.

What seems here like irrelevant vaudeville is actually an adroit piece of symbolic farce. Undershaft's mistake in taking Cusins for his "son" foreshadows the relation the Professor will bear to him at the end of the play. In addition, Cusins proceeds to dispel the confusion concerning the mixed-up introductions with an ease and self-command that does not go unnoticed by the maker of cannons. No less than Barbara and Undershaft do Cusins and Undershaft find themselves understanding each other in the midst of strangers:

UNDERSHAFT: . . . There is only one true morality for every man; but every man has not the same true morality.

LOMAX [*overtaxed*]: Would you mind saying that again? I didnt quite follow it.

CUSINS: It's quite simple. As Euripides says, one man's meat is another man's poison morally as well as physically.

UNDERSHAFT: Precisely.

LOMAX: Oh, that! Yes, yes, yes. True. True.

Lomax, Sarah, and Stephen are the nonentities in the midst of whom Barbara, Cusins, and Undershaft already form a vital triad.

In the second act, Undershaft and Cusins are left together for a few minutes at the shelter. Though Undershaft scores heavily against the sentiments proffered in the Professor's translations from Euripides, Cusins survives the onslaught by virtue of the same urbanity and detachment so characteristic of his future father-in-law. Moreover, his insistence that nothing can stop him from marrying Barbara reveals a determination that Undershaft approves of and that he cannot in any case vanquish:

> UNDERSHAFT: You mean that you will stick at nothing: not even the conversion of the Salvation Army to the worship of Dionysos.
>
> CUSINS: The business of the Salvation Army is to save, not to wrangle about the name of the pathfinder. Dionysos or another: what does it matter?
>
> UNDERSHAFT [*rising and approaching him*]: Professor Cusins: you are a young man after my own heart.
>
> CUSINS: Mr Undershaft: you are, as far as I am able to gather, a most infernal old rascal; but you appeal very strongly to my sense of ironic humor.
>
> *Undershaft mutely offers his hand. They shake.*

Undershaft has met his match—in both senses of that phrase.

But the match to result will engage Barbara as well. The determination that has been noted in both men should remind us that Barbara too has "a propensity to have her own way and order people about." If Cusins's dislike of wrangling about the name of the pathfinder strikes a responsive chord in Undershaft, it would also strike one in this young woman, who believes that the sooner men "stop calling one another names, the better." All three have a touch of fine fanaticism which can be quick at the expense of others' feelings: Undershaft's dismissal of his daughter's "tinpot tragedy," Cusins's sarcasm in reference to her "broken heart," Barbara's honest delight at Bill Walker's fate at the hands of Todger Fairmile. Furthermore, all three have that urge for inclusiveness that marks Shaw's most positive characters: Undershaft is not one to keep morals and business "in water-tight compartments," Cusins is a collector of religions who finds that he can "believe them all," and Barbara incorporates "Dionysos and all the others" in herself. And there is yet another resemblance: Undershaft's philosophy of money and gunpowder, "command of life and command of death," is (he admits) mad; Cusins is mad as a hatter because a sane man cannot translate Euripides; and as for Barbara:

> UNDERSHAFT [*seizing him by the shoulder*]: Can a sane woman make a man of a waster or a woman of a worm?
>
> CUSINS [*reeling before the storm*]: Father Colossus—Mammoth Millionaire—
>
> UNDERSHAFT [*pressing him*]: Are there two mad people or three in this Salvation shelter today?
>
> CUSINS: You mean Barbara is as mad as we are?

UNDERSHAFT [*pushing him lightly off and resuming his equanimity suddenly and completely*]: Pooh, Professor! let us call things by their proper names. I am a millionaire; you are a poet; Barbara is a savior of souls. What have we three to do with the common mob of slaves and idolaters?

Father Keegan too was "mad"—are Undershaft, Barbara, and Cusins to become the "three in one and one in three" that will turn his dream into a fact? Cusins here is the figure of potential resolution because he can see from both points of view; his sympathies are clearly with Barbara, yet he can appreciate Undershaft's materialistic premise. If the sense of powerful fusion with Cusins as the central character is not maintained in the final pages of the play, it can hardly be because the idea came to Shaw as an afterthought. It is not the preparation, but the execution, that presents the difficulty.

The second principal charge against *Major Barbara*—that Undershaft is a frivolously conceived or intellectually confused personage—usually reflects minimal engagement with the text of the play. Yet this objection does have a valid component: if Undershaft is indeed the catalyst of upward evolutionary change, why *do* audiences have such mixed feelings toward this most highly developed version of the paradigmatic Shavian hero? Even attentive readers leave the play puzzled as to whether or not the dramatist himself considers Undershaft an admirable character. The answer lies in Shaw's awareness that individualism has its perils as well as its glories. In previous chapters we have noted his perception that conventions may be violated from bad motives as well as good ones. The mystical Mrs. Knox in *Fanny's First Play* counsels that if you have inner blessedness, "the spirit will set you free to do what you want and guide you to do right"; if on the other hand inner blessedness is lacking, you had "best be respectable and stick to the ways that are marked out . . . for youve nothing else to keep you straight." To be sure, a man with "no power in him to keep him steady" is well advised to "cling to the powers outside him"; but how is a man to *know* whether he has such powers in him or not except by the exercise of fallible judgment? It is no simple matter to distinguish the genuine avatar who unites his will with the divine voice, from the imitator who (perhaps unwittingly) substitutes his own will for it. Shaw's later plays offer several sham supermen (Cain, Napoleon, the dictators in *Geneva*) who cannot activate an evolutionary leap because they fall into Peer Gynt's error of refusing to recognize that the "world-will," Life Force, or divine voice is outside as well as inside them (*QI*). The brutish Cain in *Back to Methuselah* is correct when he claims that the great man "makes the Voice respect him," but wrong when he proceeds to destroy the difficult balance between inner and outer forces by insisting that such a man finally "dictates what the Voice shall say." How to differentiate the authentic prophet who rises above the law from the enthusiast or scamp who falls below it was a problem still torturing Shaw when he included a debate between Jesus and Pilate as part of the preface to *On the Rocks* (1933):

> PILATE: . . . Your truth, as you call it, can be nothing but the thoughts for which you have found words which will take effect in deeds if I set you loose to scatter your words broadcast among the people. Your own people who bring you to me tell me that your thoughts are abominable and your words blasphemous. . . . How am I to distinguish between the blasphemies of my soldiers reported to me by my centurions and your blasphemies reported to me by your High Priest?
>
> JESUS: Woe betide you and the world if you do not distinguish!

While Christ's rejoinder is striking, it does not so much refute Pilate as draw attention to the extreme difficulty of the question he has raised. For to distinguish wrongly may mean not only to call a Christ a criminal, but also to call a criminal a Christ.

The difficulty of discriminating precisely accounts for Shaw's own ambivalence toward his hero. Undershaft is the ostensible bad man of whom it takes a Cusins to say, "Suppose he is a great man, after all!" Very well, but suppose he isn't? Shaw approaches the issue with a combination of faith and doubt arising from his awareness that the urge for what is commonly called self-transcendence is both man's noblest impulse and the source of nearly all that is most despicable in human nature. Undershaft's implicit rationale, which amounts to something like "I am pursuing raw power as an important step in an evolutionary process," could conceivably turn out to be only a more subtly rationalized self-deception than that of the patriot who thinks his country pursues such power to preserve freedom for mankind. And while few are likely so to misconstrue Shaw's meaning as to confuse Undershaft with a patriot, there is no way to prove that he is not merely aping the paradigmatic process as a means of trapping Cusins and Barbara into devoting their energies to preaching his gospel and thus destroying themselves. If Undershaft is clearly being sarcastic when he tells Mrs. Baines that he is giving the Salvation Army five thousand pounds to hasten his own "commercial ruin," then might he not also be sarcastic when he asks Cusins, "Dare you make war on war? Here are the means"? And is it possible that Cusins, who saw the irony behind appearances in Mrs. Baines's case, misses it in his own because now *his* vanity is flattered by the idea of being able to use power for a supposedly higher cause?

The occasional delight Undershaft takes in brutality—such as in the "oceans of blood" speech or the "good news from Manchuria" incident—serves to keep before the audience the possibility of a genuine malevolence in his character. "The way of life lies through the factory of death," says Cusins; but what if this sentiment should turn out to underscore a paradox instead of a synthesis? No matter how much one may admire his acumen and strength, the conviction that Undershaft is "St Andrew" rather than the "Prince of Darkness" ultimately is one of faith. The skeptical are entitled to reverse the emphasis of Barbara's assessment by concluding that God speaks through him sometimes, but he *may* be a devil.

The resulting ambiguity increases the fascination of the character by blurring his relation to the drama's schematic framework. Indeed, *Major Barbara* ceases to convince at exactly the point where Shaw loses the ability to play *against* his own thematic conception. The problem of the unsatisfactory ending—the third major charge against the play— arises from the author's emotional resistance to recognizing the full implications of his material. The character of Cusins is the nub of the problem. After striking favorable terms regarding salary, Cusins assures Barbara that his soul does not yet belong to Undershaft because "the real tug of war is still to come. What about the moral question?" Yet much of what follows seems disturbingly irrelevant to the moral question:

> CUSINS: May I not love even my father-in-law?
> UNDERSHAFT: Who wants your love, man? By what right do you take the liberty of offering it to me? I will have your due heed and respect, or I will kill you. But your love! Damn your impertinence!
> CUSINS [*grinning*]: I may not be able to control my affections, Mac.

The amusement value of such exchanges obscures their weakness in helping us to see how the Professor is being won on that "holier ground" he had earlier claimed as his territory. What real convictions Cusins has for accepting the offer appear only in the final epilogue-like scene between himself and Barbara. Here some of his more vatic utterances ("I want to make power for the world") and especially his culminating outburst ("Dare I make war on war? I dare. I must. I will") would have been more effective as irony than epiphany. As it is, one does not quite know whether it is Shaw or Cusins who is being foolish. The result is a real problem of tone. If Undershaft remains dramatically powerful because his thematic function is subordinated to his character, then Cusins evaporates because his character is sacrificed to bolster the thematic union he is supposed to embody. At that point, the play becomes a polemic. Only satire could have saved the day.

It is important to see how much was at stake for Shaw in writing this play. Having already examined the conclusions of *Man and Superman* through the dark filter of *John Bull's Other Island,* the dramatist now attempts in *Major Barbara* to clarify exactly where the vision of Don Juan went wrong. In this undertaking it must have occurred to him that Juan had been altogether too glib when he responded to Satan's indictment of humanity with the rejoinder, "Pshaw! All this is old." Lucifer's "force of Death" speech had been filled with allusions to Maxim guns, torpedo boats, bullets, explosive shells, poison gas—to the very paraphernalia of destruction commanded by Andrew Undershaft in *Major Barbara.* The death force disregarded by Juan now dominates the stage as the hero of the play; and if Barbara is unable to dismiss her father's arguments as Don Juan had dismissed Satan's, the reason is that Shaw himself has come to understand that the quest for salvation cannot be reduced to the luxury of *choosing* between heaven and hell. The example of Father Keegan would be fresh in his memory to suggest that Juan's "heavenly temperament" is no ticket to heaven, because it cannot master the half of life that is inimical to it. The "wicked side" cannot be ignored; the only hope of realizing Juan's synthesis is to incorporate the death force *within* the Life Force. Shaw's attempt to rise to this challenge made the writing of *Major Barbara* the most daring act of his artistic career; unfortunately, the desirability of the kind of synthesis the play attempts is easier to demonstrate than is its possibility. When the wise seek power, are they immune to its corrupting influences? What if the elements in conflict contain within themselves the source, not of union, but of mutual cancellation? If the oppositions with which the play deals are fundamental rather than apparent, then to urge their reconciliation is to impose a comic solution on materials that are essentially tragic.

Despite some good lines, the last few pages of *Major Barbara* comprise one of those rare scenes in which Shaw's powers of expression seem to fail him. The insistence upon affirmation leads to a forced sentimentality (Barbara cooing about her "dear little Dolly boy") as well as some regrettable rhapsodizing based on Biblical phrases. What is worse, language is used to sidestep substance. It is one thing to imply, as is done throughout the play, that one side of life cannot be separated from another—but Barbara's "life is all one" resorts to cliché to muddle the meaning of that thought. It is one matter to insist that power can be spiritual as well as material; but Cusins's "all power is spiritual" is only a paraphrase of Carlyle's disastrous aphorism "All force is moral." Surely this swelling rhetoric is strained—for all his determination in this play to confront the infernal dimension of human nature, Shaw seems reluctant to give the devil his due without also assuring us that the Prince of Darkness can be made to behave like a gentleman.

Shaw himself was never satisfied with the final act. Writing to actress Eleanor Robson, he lamented: "But oh! Eleanor, between ourselves, the play, especially in the last act, is a mere ghost; at least so it seems to me. . . . It was a fearful job: I did what I never have had to do before, threw the last act away and wrote it again. Brainwork comes natural to me; but this time I knew I was working—and now nobody understands." Further revisions made in later editions evidence his continued effort at improvement; but most of these changes were insufficient and mechanical. There could be no solution to an insoluble problem. All during his career Shaw had been exploring the theme of the union between the practical and the spiritual, fact and ideal, wisdom and power, employing in his quest the controlling metaphors of heaven and hell, salvation and damnation. The first half of his life was capped with *Man and Superman,* a great play in which he solved the problem intellectually; it was followed by *John Bull's Other Island,* in which he saw the eagerly awaited consummation destroyed by the nature of the world. Finally, in *Major Barbara* he made a culminating effort to achieve the synthesis by confronting for the first time the need for efficiency to be founded on the control of power at the most elemental level. But his drive for affirmation was so overwhelming that he was not willing to face his own growing sense that the "abyss of moral horror" admits of no transcendence, that the breach between heaven and earth is absolute, that the resulting separation is the human condition. So he presented a fantasy as real—which is to say, he idealized his theme. It was Shaw's misfortune to have sensed that his view of life was tragic at precisely the moment when he was temperamentally least capable of facing tragedy.

Shaw's Own Problem Play

J. Percy Smith

Major Barbara is to Bernard Shaw as *Measure for Measure* is to Shake-speare. Each has for its central figure a young and beautiful woman of the purest religious faith and aspiration, who is presented with a moral problem that shakes her to the heart. Each contains an accompanying set of characters who range, as do the incidents of the play, from high comedy to farce to brutality. Each represents a solution to the problem that is of questionable validity in terms of the play itself, and enigmatic as to the author's deeper intention and as to the play's moral and philosophical im-plications. Each has evoked a notable quantity of critical comment expressing widely varying views, mainly satisfactory to their authors.

   With few exceptions, the critics who saw the first performance of *Major Barbara* in 1905 found it too long and ultimately puzzling. Some found it offensive because of Barbara's utterance, in act 2, of the agonized words of Jesus on the cross, and because of the brutality displayed when in the same Act the ruffian Bill Walker flings down the Salvation Army lass Jenny Hill and punches her in the face. The notion of blasphemy having become as quaint to modern audiences as Shake-spearian references to chastity, and the presence of brutality virtually a *sine qua non,* recent writers have rightly ignored those early objections and turned to the larger issues, not without a wary eye on the preface. The growing body of critical discussion attests to the troublesome, even ambiguous, quality of the final effect of the play.

From *English Studies in Canada* 4, no. 4 (Winter 1978). © 1978 by the Association of Canadian University Teachers of English.

Not all the critics are troubled. J. L. Wisenthal sees *Major Barbara* as an assertion of "the necessity of accepting and combining good and evil, heaven and hell." His proposition that such a "marriage of contraries" is the theme of the play is held by some others: for example, Robert R. Speckhard, who gives the marriage a Jungian blessing by envisaging Andrew Undershaft as the Doctor/Cook, a magic demon whose "magic is modern magic; the inherent power for good of modern technology: its ability to transform our cities into places fresh and clean and beautiful." Some see the play in terms of conversion rather than marriage: the conversion of Barbara from Christianity to something else—a conversion which, says Maurice Valency, is "like Captain Brassbound's, a matter of turning from illusion to reality." For Charles Frankel the play presents a "remarkably straightforward espousal of the morality of Power" based on the classic "reasons of Machiavelli and Hobbes and Marx and Nietzsche," followed by an appeal for a "relativistic and provisional view of human ideals." Fred Mayne likewise sees it as "an attempt to reconcile the saint and the realist," but he goes on to say that "it is a spurious reconciliation as Shaw seems to realize when he makes Cusins . . . the chief object of the campaign for conversion."

I propose to examine the reasons underlying the critical difficulties that *Major Barbara* presents, considering first the principal sources of the play and then the ambivalence in Shaw's attitude to the central moral question that it raises.

Shaw himself gave at least two different accounts of the origins of *Major Barbara*. He told his biographer Henderson before 1911 that he had long "had the idea of the religious play in mind; and I always saw it as a conflict between the economic and religious views of life." He went on to say that the particular circumstance that caused the play to take form was his acquaintance with a young playwright named Charles McEvoy:

> At the close of the war between the States in America [Shaw told Henderson], Mr. McEvoy's father, who had fought on the side of the Confederacy, and was a most gentle and humane man, established a factory for the manufacture of torpedoes and various high-power explosives. The idea of this grey haired gentleman, of peculiarly gentle nature and benignant appearance, manufacturing the most deadly instruments for the destruction of his fellow creatures ap-

pealed to Shaw as the quintessence of ironic contrast. Here, of course, we have the germ idea of Andrew Undershaft.

On the whole, however, Shaw seems to have preferred an account that placed the origins of the play in his early sympathetic relations with the Salvation Army, which began through his sharing their interest in both street-corner preaching and lively music. In an interview that he gave just before the revival of *Major Barbara* in 1929, he told how he had been "struck by the dramatic power of some of the Salvation Army lasses . . . and by the excellent quality of their bands." He had suggested that if the dramatically gifted lasses

> could have little plays written for them the effect would be greater than that of the dramatic songs which they sang, and I offered to provide them with a sample or two of what I meant. . . . In the end it was clear that my proposal only embarrassed the Army, so I went ahead with it myself, and "Major Barbara" was the result.

The two accounts do not contradict each other; we may assume that each contains some truth about the origins of the play. There were, however, other sources, in particular two in literature, both so unrelievedly tragical that one wonders how Shaw could have thought he might turn them to comedy.

The first is the legend of Barbara, the virgin martyr and saint (at least until her very recent discreditation), and it is curious that, save for one brief note, no critic seems to have referred to that legend in relation to Shaw's play, nor did he himself mention it. The playlet called *The Glimpse of Reality, a Tragedietta,* which he wrote in 1909 but left unpublished until 1926, contains repeated references to St Barbara, but they are not relevant to the earlier play.

She was one of the most popular medieval saints, except in England, where, if one may judge by the comparative dearth of literary references to her and churches dedicated to her, she received little attention. Her story, as told in Butler's *Lives of the Saints* (the account being drawn from Caxton's version of the *Golden Legend*), concerns the daughter of "a rich man, a paynim, which adored and worshipped idols, which man was named Dioscorus." Dioscorus kept his daughter, Barbara, in "a high and strong tower . . . to the end that no man should see her because of her great beauty." Nevertheless there were princely suitors; but Barbara rejected angrily her father's suggestion that she consider marriage. Leaving her thus confined, Dioscorus went on a long journey. In his absence, Barbara affirmed the Trinity by ordering workmen who were building a bath-house that her father had commissioned, to insert three windows in it rather than two. She was then baptized by a holy man, received the Holy Ghost, and "became marvellously subtle and clear in the love of Jesus Christ." She proceeded to deface the idols worshipped by her father. When he returned he was furious, demanded an explanation, and took her before a judge, who, after hearing her case, gave her an ultimatum: "Now choose whether ye will spare yourself and offer to the gods, or else die by cruel torments." Barbara remained faithful to Jesus Christ. Dioscorus therefore, after torturing her in an effort to break her faith, took her onto a mountain and beheaded both her and her companion, Juliana. Immediately thereafter, Dioscorus was consumed utterly by fire from heaven.

There are additional details; and there are other versions of the story. The early *Studia Sinaitica* "Select Narratives of Holy Women," the English translation of which appeared in 1900, presents a somewhat different version, as does the popular mystery play at Laval in France, which in the year 1493 required six days for its presentation. But the basic story is the same: a beautiful young virgin is converted to belief in Jesus, her pagan father being absent. On his return, he demands that she renounce her new religion and return to his. When she will not do so, he kills her and is then himself killed by lightning. In 1905, the year of Shaw's play, there appeared the third impression of Mrs Anna Jameson's *Sacred and Legendary Art,* first published in 1848. Mrs Jameson told the story of St Barbara, adding that she was said to have been a woman of unusually independent and original mind who arrived at her religion virtually by her own study and meditation, the holy man who baptized her having been sent by Origen when she wrote him for advice. Mrs Jameson pointed to another long tradition about Barbara: she was "patron saint of armorers and gunsmiths: of firearms and fortifications. She is invoked against thunder and lightning, and all accidents arising from explosions of gunpowder." Mrs Jameson's chief concern was with the saint as a subject for artists, and she mentioned many of the best-known treatments of her in painting and sculpture.

As the dates suggest, Shaw could have encountered the legend in any or all of these places, or in others. Caxton's version of the *Golden Legend* was printed by William Morris at the Kelmscott Press in September 1892—a year in which Shaw spent a good deal of time, including Christmas, at Kelmscott. On the other hand, he had acquired a considerable knowledge of religious paintings in the churches and galleries of Europe and must have seen many representations of St Barbara. One detail not mentioned in any of the works that I have referred to suggests still another possibility: in 1904 Agnes Dunbar noted in her *Dictionary of Saintly Women* that St Barbara had long been regarded by some scholars as the Christian personification of Bellona, the goddess of war. That Shaw's Barbara should be an officer in a quasi-military church is fitting.

At all events, it is clear that he was familiar with the legend. Like other stories of religious martyrs—Becket, More, Joan of Arc—it comprises essentially tragic material, whatever the outcome in eternity may have been. Shaw was not only aware of this fact, but of its peculiar insistence as he wrote his play; for in the conversation with Henderson to which I have referred, he said: "I have shown the conflict between the naturally religious soul, Barbara, and Undershaft, with his gospel of money, of force, of power. . . . The tragedy results from the collision of Undershaft's philosophy with Barbara's." The word "tragedy" is significant. Shaw did not usually apply it to *Major Barbara,* nor intend the play to be regarded as tragical.

What then of the play in relation to the legend? In *Major Barbara* Shaw presents a beautiful young woman, the daughter of a rich munitions-manufacturer—manifestly a "paynim." In the course of a long absence of his, she has been converted to belief in Jesus, by a route that leads her fiancé Cusins to say that she is "quite original in her religion" and has given herself ardently to the Salvation Army's way of worship and work: the exuberant joy of music, preaching, and prayer; the patient practice, not without anxiety and pain, of charitable works. When her father returns and finds her following her new faith, he deliberately sets out to subvert it, not by cutting off her head, but rather by paralysing her heart. In a passage in which his manner is described as successively contemptuous, cold, and sardonic, he asserts his intention: "Barbara must belong to us, not to the Salvation Army." He proceeds not by physical assault or philosophical argument, but by the devices that long experience has taught him how to use with perfect assurance. He simply launches a commercial transaction, with unfeeling calculation. He first proposes that Barbara accept his faith instead of hers—his religion of money and gunpowder—the proposal taking the form not of words but of a proffered gift of money. Barbara, understanding the intent well enough, refuses flatly: "Two million millions would not be enough. There is bad blood on your hands; and nothing but good blood can cleanse them. Money is no use. Take it away." Undershaft finds, however, as he knew he would, that the Army is not of Barbara's mind: it accepts his cheque with a prayer of thanksgiving "that the Army is saved, and through you," as the Commissioner says with unintended irony. At that point Shaw departs from the essentials of the legend, then turns its ending around: for Barbara, instead of being haled before a judge, is herself made to judge; she goes with her father onto a hill to review the evidence, and, having judged, she capitulates; with the result that although at the end of the play she is described as having "gone right up into the skies," with not only God's work to do but very comfortable circumstances in which to do it, and marriage and wealth as her lot, it is her father to whom Shaw was to refer—in the preface that he subsequently wrote—as a saint. Undershaft talked of buying the Army, but he has in fact bought Barbara; for the effect of the transaction is that she abandons the religion that she knew in the Army and joins him. She may, as she says, "die with the colours"; but the blood and fire that she knew have undergone an elemental change.

Shaw has, then, taken the tragic saint's legend and given it a modern application and a "happy" ending, with a clear victory for the "economic" over the "religious" view of life. To say that, however, is to oversimplify vastly the character of Andrew Undershaft. A mere money-handler would not have imposed on Barbara. If the "collision of philosophies" is to have dramatic substance, Undershaft must be provided with a philosophical force and a personality strong enough to make Barbara's overthrow convincing, her final decision understandable. To achieve this effect, Shaw drew again on tragic material, his indebtedness to which and to its translator he acknowledged in a program note. Some aspects of the debt have been studied; some need further exploration.

One of the ways in which Shaw departs from the legend of the saint is in giving Barbara a successful suitor, the intellectual Adolphus Cusins. Cusins is not a convert, but a "collector of religions," who, as Barbara's mother, Lady Britomart, says, "pretends to be a Salvationist, and actually plays the drum for her in public because he has fallen head over ears in love with her." Cusins's original was of course Shaw's friend Professor Gilbert Murray. On his way to becoming the best-known Greek scholar of his time, Murray had tried his hand at writing plays, just when Shaw was beginning his career as a dramatist. In

1892, the year in which *Widowers' Houses* was first performed, Murray wrote *Carolyn Sahib,* which Shaw read and admired. Doubtless he also read Murray's brief introductory note to the published version, in 1900, in which he said: "I do not think I should chafe at the appearance [ie, in a play] of a villanous [sic] Professor of Greek."

He was to have ample opportunity to test his ability to withstand chafing, for Shaw involved not only him but his wife and mother-in-law in *Major Barbara.* The story of that involvement has been told and much of its significance examined, especially by Sidney P. Albert. A most cultivated humanist, Murray gave Shaw good-natured, sensitive counsel about the play. He must have found it difficult not to chafe over Cusins, for even half a century later he remarked that "that unprincipled young man does not in my own judgment seem particularly like me."

Still, there are other aspects of the indebtedness beyond Murray's criticisms and the character of Cusins. When Shaw wrote *Major Barbara,* Murray had given up writing plays and turned to doing those verse translations that were to transform classical Greek plays, especially those of Euripides, from "the blackest of curses of the public school system," as Masefield called them, to winners of notable success in the London theatre, and eventually to incur the condescending strictures of T. S. Eliot. Shaw gave Murray's work as translator and producer his enthusiastic approval. In *Major Barbara* Cusins quotes a score of lines from the translation of Euripides' last play, *The Bacchae,* which Murray had published in 1902. That play provided more than lines for Cusins, however: it complemented the legend of St Barbara by supplying a central figure of superhuman force, and a pagan faith to be held by the heroine's father and set against her own.

The Bacchae deals with the story of how the god Dionysos comes to Thebes to establish his religion, only to find that the Thebans, led by their king Pentheus, have scorned him and mocked his birth. In anger, Dionysos brings madness to the Theban women and sends them out of the city to celebrate his rites. Then, after some discourse with Pentheus and a series of episodes culminating in the king's entering the scene dressed as a Bacchic devotee and manifestly intoxicated (if not with wine, then with some other Dionysian infusion), he brings it about that Pentheus is killed by the Theban women, for they find that he has been spying on their celebrations from a lofty pine tree. A messenger reports how they have seized him and torn his body apart; and his head is carried onto the scene by his mother, who in her madness supposes him to be a lion that they have killed. The cessation of their madness brings on them horror and repentance for their apostasy to Dionysos, for which, however, there is no forgiveness. Dionysos exiles them from Thebes, then vanishes on a cloud.

In the introductory note to his translation, Murray reminded his readers that Dionysos was the son of the mortal Semele and the god Zeus, and that when the pregnant Semele begged Zeus to appear before her in his glory, he did so in a flash of lightning that killed her in the same moment that it caused her to give premature birth to Dionysos, after which the infant was mysteriously nourished by Zeus himself until a second and miraculous birth occurred. Murray pointed out also that Dionysos was originally "a god of the common folk, despised and unauthorized [but] eventually so strong as to be adopted into the Olympian hierarchy"; and that he was "a god of Intoxication, of Inspiration, a giver of superhuman or immortal life"—in short, a powerful fertility god. Finally, he noted that the more primitive form of Dionysian religion had eventually been profoundly affected by the reforms of Orphism, which, "ascetic, mystical, ritualistic and emotional . . . easily excited both enthusiasm and ridicule."

Murray did not here comment on the play as a whole, though he must surely have done so in the course of his conversations with Shaw when *Major Barbara* was in progress. He was to state his view in a letter to Lillah McCarthy, when she was preparing to enact the role of Dionysos in 1908:

> Try to imagine what the story of some persecuted Christian saint or missionary would be, if it were continued into the next world and we saw the persecutors in a mediaeval hell being torn with red hot pincers while the saint, with a seraphic smile, stood by saying, "I told you so." Think even of the Crucifixion story as treated with Pontius Pilate in hell suffering ghastly tortures while Jesus stood by making comments. That gives one almost exactly the point of the *Bacchae*. It is exactly the criticism that Euripides would have made on an ordinary mediaeval mystery play. "You say that blasphemous people suffer in hell? Very well, I represent them doing so; now see if you admire your God who has made a hell." Pentheus is tyrant and persecutor, Dionysus a holy and sanctified being; but when this holy being has his will, his full revenge, he seems infinitely worse than his persecutor.

The father of Major Barbara was of unknown if not mysterious birth, a foundling, who came from the common people, knew poverty. He had what amounted to a remarkable second birth when he seized the opportunity to be rich and powerful and became heir to the Undershaft munitions empire. The name he then assumed was adopted from the Parish Church of St Andrew Undershaft, in London, where, as its illustrious parishioner John Stow wrote in the sixteenth century, there was erected annually through many decades a maypole that overtopped the church tower and served as a centre of springtime (Stow does not call them Dionysian) activities until a wave of puritanism, stirred by a particularly forceful if somewhat bizarre preacher, caused it to be destroyed. Andrew Undershaft returns to his family after long absence, to find his daughter practising a religion that challenges his own, and being abetted by her fiancé. By the exercise of his power in response to that challenge, he brings her to his own faith and makes the fiancé his heir. In that exercise of power he is joined by his true partner and *alter ego*—not his business partner Lazarus, but Bodger the distiller. Bodger is not necessary to the play and never appears in it; but Dionysus was a god of intoxication as well as power. Indeed, the manuscript of the play shows that Shaw repeatedly wrote "Bacchus" in the first instance, then substituted "Dionysos."

There is no lack of parallels with and explicit references to Dionysos (at least as he appears in *The Bacchae*) in *Major Barbara*. Cusins does not at first recognize the Dionysian quality of Undershaft, as Pentheus did not recognize the god in the Stranger who came to Thebes. Gradually, however, he is stirred by Undershaft's force, and as the second act of the play proceeds he addresses him successively, with growing excitement, as "Father Colossus—Mammoth Millionaire—," then as "Mephistopheles! Machiavelli!" and finally, after an excited drum obbligato, cries, "Dionysos Undershaft has descended! I am possessed!" Later, Undershaft becomes for him "The Prince of Darkness," but the epithet is one of admiration, and Cusins's acceptance of Undershaft is complete. He tells Barbara, on the morning after his conversion, that Dionysos not only made him drunk, but "sat there and completed the wreck of my moral basis, the rout of my convictions, the purchase of my soul." His mocking description of the Salvation Army meeting that he and Undershaft have attended suggests the power of Dionysos to make people mad: "It was an amazing meeting. Mrs Baines almost died of emotion, Jenny Hill simply gibbered with hysteria. The Prince of Darkness played his trombone like a madman: its brazen roarings laughter of the damned. 117 conversions took place then

ɔgether, the legend of the Christian saint who was to become patroness of armourers, and the Euripidean play about the god of power and intoxication, provide the essential material out of which *Major Barbara* was shaped. The saint's father, the brutal Dioscorus, has become the Dionysian Undershaft, able to overthrow his daughter's faith and bring her to the side of the armourers. By what processes of the dramatist's imagination the two sets of material grew together we cannot of course know. Clearly, too, there were other "sources": Lady Britomart and her family constitute one of Shaw's many debts to Oscar Wilde, for example. Nevertheless, although various writers have argued that the play shows the influence of Nietzsche, Ibsen, and others, it seems to me that Shaw was quite right in warning his critics, in the first section of his preface, against listening for a Nietzschean or Ibsenite or other leitmotif in every Shavian aria.

One other important "source" is readily identifiable. The particular moral problem with which Barbara is confronted in act 2, the treatment of which leads her to capitulate to her father, is not to be found in either the saint's legend or *The Bacchae,* but in Shaw's own experience. William Archer, reviewing *Major Barbara* in December 1905, argued that since the play in no way represents a picture of life, it must be an allegory, typifying, he supposed, "the superiority of selection over hereditary succession as a means of securing competent men to carry on the work of the world." He found act 2 especially allegorical, though of what he did not know, and he proceeded to argue with some justice that the play is less about religion than about morality and to call it a "morality play." Doing so, he pointed to an issue that was certainly in Shaw's mind, though Archer did not explore its larger significance. Commenting on the central episode—the acceptance by the Salvation Army of Undershaft's and Bodger's money after Barbara has refused it—Archer asserted that Barbara does not in fact reason out her problem: "She is simply paralysed by the discovery that the Salvation Army does not sniff at every coin proffered to it."

Shaw must have understood Archer's reference well enough. Twenty years before he wrote *Major Barbara,* he had been aghast at the acceptance by the Social Democratic Federation of an election contribution that the Tories had made to it in the hope of reducing the threat of a Liberal victory. The SDF leader, H. M. Hyndman, had dismissed the protests that were made against accepting the "Tory gold" with the shrugging classical comment, *"Non olet."* Shaw, how-ever, was outraged: "The Federation [he wrote, in a letter] are con-victed of offering to sell their fictitious numbers to the highest bidder (in money, not reforms). . . . All England is satisfied that we are a paltry handful of blackguards." Seven years later, he wrote that he thought Hyndman's retort a sufficient one. Yet when he wrote the *Plan of Campaign for Labour* (Fabian Tract no. 49) in 1894, he referred again to the "Tory gold" and said the temptation to take it "must be resisted on the ground of expediency *even by those who cannot see any principle at stake*" (my italics). He saw, then, a principle at stake, the principle raised by this question: Is it morally justifiable to accept the fruit of continuing activities that we regard as evil, in order to achieve ends that we regard as good? The word "continuing" is important as expressing what Shaw meant when he referred to the bribe taking the form of money, not reforms. For though Archer criticizes Barbara for not reasoning out her problem, the play makes it clear that she under-stands it very well. While she has been holding out for repentance as the necessary condition of the salvation of Bill Walker and the accep-tance of his money, the Army reveals itself as quite ready to accept gifts even from its most deadly enemies, and even when by accepting those gifts, as both Barbara and her father make very clear, it shows that it not only cares nothing about the repentance of those enemies but actually abets their activitites.

At this point in the play Barbara's attitude resembles that of Jesus as he talked with the rich ruler and told him that if he wished to be saved he must get rid of his riches—all of them. Jesus's concern in doing so was not mainly with the poor, but with the young man's soul; as Barbara's concern is with the soul of Bill Walker. The Army, however—unlike Barbara, who even before meeting him expressed her interest in her father's soul—shows virtually no interest in the souls of Undershaft and Bodger, only in their money. When Barbara takes off her Salvation Army pin and gives it to her father, whose momentarily reluctant acceptance of it has the tacit approval of the Commissioner, Mrs Baines, she is dramatizing what both she and Undershaft under-stand: he has "bought" the Army, in a directly financial transaction. No wonder he goes off to celebrate his Dionysian rites to the exuber-ant murmur of Cusins's aside as he hands him a trombone: "Blow, Machiavelli, blow." No wonder Barbara cries out in anguish: "Drunk-enness and Murder! My God: why hast thou forsaken me?"

Shaw is not here caricaturing the Army. He had been at some

pains to ensure that his play would not be offensive to that body, although when Commissioner Nicol was asked to comment on it shortly after its opening, he said that while he had not seen it (though some of his colleagues had), he was of the opinion that Barbara's only resemblance to a Salvation Army lass was in her spirit of self sacrifice, and that he himself "would refuse money from none; I would take it even from His Satanic Majesty." W. T. Stead, writing in the *Review of Reviews,* said: "I tried to draw General Booth or his Chief of Staff about 'Major Barbara,' but they declined. Neither of them had seen it, and the chief, from what he has heard of it, does not exactly like it."

At all events, at the end of act 2 *Major Barbara* is what Shaw called it in his conversation with Henderson: a tragedy. It has grown out of tragic material, and has taken the shape and the course that the material required: the rich pagan father has destroyed the saintly daughter whose religion challenged his; the god has asserted his divine authority, claimed his sacrifice, possessed those on whom he has descended.

Shaw's mind was set against tragedy, however; *Major Barbara* could no more be without its final act, in which the tragedy is obscured or obliterated (according to one's view of the outcome) than *Saint Joan* could be without its epilogue. The struggle that he had in writing act 3 has been recounted by Sidney P. Albert and need not be reviewed here. Not surprisingly, the play has ceased to be Barbara's. It has become Undershaft's, with Cusins also playing a role more central than hers. Barbara, after what she felt to be a desolating betrayal by the Army of its central teaching—acceptance of Jesus and salvation through him by repentance and faith—and of herself, is shown the bright, clean company town of Perivale St Andrews, and with breath-taking accommodation of mind and resilience of spirit comes to the view that the end—the opportunity to do God's work "for its own sake"—justifies the means by which the community is sustained, those means being vividly represented by the dummy soldiers surrounding her, mutilated and resembling grotesque corpses, as Shaw's directions say.

The question of ends and means had been dealt with by Shaw in other contexts. In 1900, five years before *Major Babara* appeared, he had made a speech that is interesting for readers of the play. The formal subject was vivisection, which he roundly condemned, arguing that the fact that an intended objective was good did not justify the pursuit of it by wrongful means:

You do not settle whether an experiment is justified or not merely by showing that it is of some use. If that were the only thing to be considered, we should kill our soldiers and sailors in time of peace simply to find out what our new guns and explosives could do.

He proceeded, enlarging the argument:

Once allow irresponsible persons an absolute right to spread torture and death all around them, if only they will promise you the millennium, and you will be landed in dynamite in Politics, just as you are already landed in vivisection in Science. The question is one of human character: you have got to make up your minds whether you will live honorably or not.

He added: "I dogmatically postulate humaneness as a condition of worthy personal character." He was to argue in that vein many times throughout his life—in regard to some subjects. In 1938, in a letter to the *New Statesman and Nation,* he pointed out the possibility of arguing "that the permanent alleviation of human suffering matters more, in the long run, than the life of a baby," and commented: "Once let loose that sort of argument and it will carry you straight to hell before you know where you are."

Unless we are to view the ending of *Major Barbara* as completely ironical (in which case most critics of the play are hopelessly in error about it), it is impossible to reconcile it with such arguments as these. The millennial Perivale St Andrews has its base exactly on the presumed right of persons to spread torture and death. Its spokesman, Undershaft, has no compunctions about asserting that right. "*I* am the government of your country," he says with a touch of brutality, to his son Stephen. And as the government of the country, he will sell arms unashamedly to whoever will pay for them. The more destructive they are, the better he is pleased, for the more he will sell. He is far beyond that stage of poverty that had brought him to saying, "Thou shalt starve ere I starve," itself a precise statement of the principle of survival that in other contexts Shaw most abhorred. Undershaft may continue to think it his maxim and to commend it to others; but his maxim long ago became the unstated one: Thou shalt be killed ere I shall be less than a millionaire answerable to no one. Maurice Valency declares that "Undershaft militant is a danger to all the world, but

Undershaft triumphant is a benevolent deity shared by all." Except, no doubt, the victims of his aerial battleships, and their friends. Barbara Bellow Watson sees in Undershaft one who has "taken a step in the direction of saving the world's honor." I like not such grinning honour; it heads Don Juan's list of the seven deadly virtues.

Although Shaw, in the passages that I have quoted, may seem to have rejected war as a means to anything, his attitude to it throughout his life was ambiguous, and the notion—held even by one editor of *Major Barbara*—that he was "a known crusader against war and destruction" will not stand close scrutiny, despite his occasional references to the unsavoury nature of Undershaft's trade. Unquestionably, with one part of his nature he hated war and destructiveness. Yet in 1900 he had argued that while the Boer War ought not to have broken out it must, once begun, be carried through to victory, since where there are "such mighty forces as gold-fields" a Great Power (in this case the British Empire) "must govern in the interests of civilization as a whole." The failure to formulate a policy that would ensure that when the Great Powers settled the East or Africa, they should take with them "a reasonable standard of life" had led Great Britain to be "so invariably bested by the old-fashioned dynastic imperialism of Russia, which by ruthless governmental energy and pioneering grit has taken the northern half of the continent of Asia whilst we have been shirking our manifest destiny in South Africa." Of manifest destiny in China, where the Boxer rising was threatening British interests, he wrote:

> The war in China is part of a series of inevitable wars for the establishment of an international level of civilization. If the Western level of civilization gets reduced by the passions which war excites to the level of refractory civilization which it attacks, the world-force which is flinging the West on the East will vanish; and the victory will be to the hardiest and skillfullest slayer.

As if it would not be so in any case. "The State which obstructs international civilization will have to go, be it big or little," he said in *Fabianism and the Empire*. He was to repeat the argument decades later in support of Mussolini's assault on Ethiopia, and in opposition to the application of sanctions against Italy by the League of Nations.

When he concluded the first draft of *Major Barbara,* in September

1905, Shaw wrote the following note on one of several blank leaves that remained in his notebook:

> This is England's real belief, if not, why your armaments. The devil of it is that we go on believing one thing and saying another; so that we never get our policy discussed. When we intend murder we discuss Christianity. When we intend piracy and conquest, we discuss our national honour. Far better to discuss what we are really doing: we should then find our bearings and make something out of it, instead of being catspaws for capitalists as we were in South Africa.

It is a strange reflection for the author of the Manifesto, who moreover was to argue within a few months that he thought Undershaft was right.

Shaw's attitude to war has been studied at some length by G. A. Pilecki and need not be reviewed further here. My point is not that there are inconsistencies in his thinking (a point not worth making) but that in *Major Barbara* he takes up the problem of ends and means in a context as to the larger implications of which he is profoundly ambivalent; and that having written two acts of a remarkable play, in which he has developed a statement of the problem that is (despite Archer's strictures) straightforward, convincing, and deeply moving, he proceeds to a solution in the third act that has none of these qualities, but lets him and everyone else off the hook as enigmatically as Shakespeare lets everyone off in *Measure for Measure*.

The instrument that he uses is of course Andrew Undershaft—undoubtedly, as Margery Morgan has said, one of his most impressive characters. Yet for all his dynamic energy, directness, self-possession and power, Undershaft is a rascal—of Falstaffian proportions, it is true, but yet a rascal. He is beyond good and evil in the same way as Sir John, albeit his tastes are different: the labels describing actions matter nothing to him if the actions themselves serve his purposes. Shaw, who often served the cause of truth by insisting that grim realities should not be allowed to hide behind pleasant-sounding tags, plays with labels himself when he discusses Undershaft in his preface and invites us to regard his conduct not as "opulent villainy" but as "energetic enterprise."

Still, by the sheer force of his mind and personality, his energy and rhetoric, Undershaft sweeps Barbara and Cusins (and, if we are not careful, ourselves) into his camp. Barbara has been at the brink of a kind of martyrdom in an experience of spiritual anguish; but within a few hours of it she unprotestingly accepts her father's brusque dismissal of her "tinpot tragedy" and prepares to go on saving souls in a society as cruel as the one she leaves, albeit its victims are out of sight. From her Salvation Army life, which in retrospect she describes as escape "from the world into a paradise of enthusiasm and prayer and soul-saving," the money for which came from Undershaft and Bodger, she is now to enter a paradise, certainly cleaner and better fed than the West Ham Shelter, of praying and soul-saving (the enthusiasm is less apparent), the money for which comes from precisely the same source. It follows that Shaw's claim in the preface that Barbara's "return to the colours" will "lead to something hopefuller" does not bear examination. Undershaft's statement of what salvation means in his empire, a few minutes after he has received news from Manchuria of the superior destructiveness of his aerial battleship, is nearer the mark:

> I will drag his soul back again to salvation for you [he says of Bill Walker, the "half-saved ruffian of West Ham"]. Not by words and dreams; but by thirty-eight shillings a week, a sound house in a handsome street, and a permanent job. In three weeks he will have a fancy waistcoat; in three months a tall hat and a chapel sitting; before the end of the year he will shake hands with a duchess at a Primrose League meeting, and join the Conservative Party.

Just as Barbara is overwhelmed by Undershaft, so is Cusins, though his soul has been purchased, as he himself says, before act 3 begins. He makes a show of resistance, and initially he finds offensive the business of making war materials—until Undershaft asks him the artful question that has comforted some otherwise troubled critics: "Dare you make war on war?" That challenge finally brings Cusins into the Undershaft empire. No doubt he seriously believes that he will be able to make war on war, though he gives no indication of how he will do so beyond vague references to wanting to "make power for the world." In any case, how seriously can we take Cusins? Shaw told Murray that he quite deliberately made him "the reverse of the theatrical strong man," wanting him to "go on his quality alone." Having that objective, he may have under-estimated the extent to which he achieved it, unconsciously impelled by his habitual deep scorn for the quality of academics. "Now let me tell you [he had once written Murray] that every university professor is an ass, and that you, like any common man, are subject to this inexorable law." A joke, of course; and so is Cusins. Shaw told an American producer, in 1928: "Cusins is easy for any clever actor who has ever seen the original. . . . The next best model is perhaps Harold Lloyd." His advice to the actor who was first to play Undershaft was different: "Undershaft is diabolically subtle, gentle, self-possessed, powerful, stupendous, as well as amusing and interesting. There are the makings of ten Hamlets and six Othellos in his mere leavings." Can any candid reader or spectator seriously believe that Cusins, the "collector of religions" whose soul was completely purchased by Undershaft in one encounter, will "give the common man weapons against the intellectual man" or "force the intellectual oligarchy to use its genius for the common good?" Shaw himself had no faith in the common man's political ability in any case when he wrote *Major Barbara*. In *Fabianism and the Empire* he had roundly declared: "The [English] masses are still in so deplorable a condition that democracy . . . is clearly contradictory to common sense," a view that he had come to through years of Fabian lecturing and permeating. Certainly Undershaft, who remembers his life as one of the common people, has no illusions about the effectiveness of Cusins's idealism: the will that runs the Undershaft industry will run Cusins in spite of himself. His last words to Cusins, which comprise the final line of the play—"Six o'clock tomorrow morning, Euripides"—are crisp, assured, conclusive in every sense. Even intellectually, Cusins is no match for Undershaft, except when they discuss the details of his own salary. (Perhaps it is his success here that gives academic critics faith in him.) Determined "realist" that he is, Undershaft does not linger for a moment over a trifling pecuniary defeat or over his own rhetorical triumphs; he sweeps on without pausing to the next item on the agenda. His culminating question about ending war by making war struck a rhetorical note that was to be echoed repeatedly through two world wars, and for the reader of 1978, when the two most formidable patrons of Undershaft's industry are reduced to calculating which of them is in a position to destroy the other and the world totally the largest number of times, it has ceased even to be ironical. It serves Undershaft's purpose, however, and having completed with it his snaring of Cusins, he gives it no more thought. Shaw knew Undershaft's Dionysian quality, and told Murray that it would be "unnatural" if Barbara and Cusins, romantic young innocents, could cope with him. Moreover, he said, he was of the view that Undershaft was in the right: being the engine-driver on the train that is society is better than being an idle passenger—as if there were no other choices, even if the analogy were more apt than it is.

The play ends with the Undershaft empire perfectly secure, as to its current profits and its future course, and with Barbara happily persuaded that she has come to a higher order of soul-saving. It is at best an enigmatic ending, its one convincing element being the overwhelming presence of Andrew Undershaft. In a letter to Shaw in 1903, Murray had expressed his admiration for *Man and Superman,* and his uneasiness about it: "It makes on me, in general, the same kind of impression as *Caesar and Cleopatra,* of an extraordinarily good thing gone wrong somehow." He accused Shaw of lacking moral courage (an accusation for which he subsequently made amends) and went on to say: "This damnable vice is intimately connected with another, which you share with Ruskin, Carlyle, and I think, Tolstoi: a fundamental preference for rhetoric to truth." What it was in *Man and Superman* that went wrong, he did not say; but his comment on Shaw's rhetoric is a discerning one. In *Major Barbara* the advantage of rhetoric is obviously given to Undershaft. In the energy, swiftness, dexterity, and wit of his debating skill, his range from thundering denunciation to contemptuous dismissal to exuberant declamation, his rhetoric is breathless, even as Shaw's was. It is not surprising that Cusins is swept away by it.

Yet, at least in this instance, the real-life professor is right. As a classicist, Murray might well have pointed Shaw to the *Gorgias,* where Socrates examines the nature and purpose of rhetoric. Before long, the examination becomes in part a discussion of the nature of power, for Socrates understood well, as modern communications experts and advertisers do, that rhetoric is an instrument of power. It is so in *Major Barbara.* Power itself, in the form of gunpowder, is a subject for discussion there, and the argument presented—with much rhetoric—is that power is morally neutral: you cannot have it for good without having it for evil also. Shaw liked to follow such an argument, as he does in the preface to this play, with a reference to "the Kantian test" for conduct, though it is rather a Shavian test, for he somewhat misrepresents Kant, and in any case is surprisingly uncritical about his precept.

What Socrates came to in the *Gorgias,* and Jesus in the incident with the rich ruler, is that the possession of power, whether in the form of wealth or in other forms, is almost certain in the long run to be destructive of its possessor's integrity. Socrates, after saying that "it is among the most powerful that you find the superlatively wicked," eventually conceded that "there is nothing to prevent good men from finding a place even among the powerful," and succeeded in naming *one* who did so. Jesus did not offer his hearers a similar example, but assured them (with a rueful smile, perhaps) that with God all things are possible. It remained for Lord Acton, like Gilbert Murray an academic, to put the blunt truth not long before Shaw wrote *Major Barbara:* Power tends to corrupt. It is a truth that Shaw, who admired successively Lenin, Mussolini, Stalin, and for a brief time Hitler, never comprehended. Had he done so, *Major Barbara* would have been a different play.

Shaw has many times been compared with Euripides, both by classicists and by people of the theatre. Sybil Thorndike, who was Barbara in the 1929 revival of *Major Barbara* and again in a film version, made this comment in a discussion of Murray's theatrical achievement:

> It does seem possible that Shaw planned *Major Barbara* as a Euripidean drama leading to a dilemma of which the only logical solution was the taking over of the armament industry by the proletariat, and then provided an ironic solution through the intervention of the goddess Aphrodite in the form of Barbara's love for Cusins. If so, the idea got lost in the torrent of Undershaft's eloquence in the last act.

In *The Bacchae* Euripides was more honest with his materials, and therefore more consistent and dramatically more sound. For *The Bacchae,* as T. B. L. Webster says, "ends with complete devastation and no hope." At the end of act 2, *Major Barbara* is approaching near to Euripidean tragedy. Given the materials with which he had chosen to work and his deep perplexity over the central moral problem of the play, not even Shaw, with all his zestful creativity and rhetoric, could turn it convincingly to comedy.

Shaw's Comedy of Disillusionment

Stanton B. Garner, Jr.

UNDERSHAFT: *You have learnt something. That always feels at first as
if you had lost something.*
BARBARA: *Well, take me to the factory of death; and let me learn something
more. There must be some truth or other behind all this frightful irony.*

A number of years ago, the *New Yorker* printed a remarkable cartoon,
at once ludicrous and poignant. It consisted of a snowman, assembled
with more eagerness than skill, stick arms propped awkwardly in its
sides. Leaning slightly forward, it stared into the middle distance with
an expression of alarm and despair. As the cartoon's caption explained
it: "The snowman realizes what he is."

Frozen both physically and spiritually in its icebound *anagnorisis,*
the snowman enacts a gaze which lies at the heart of Western drama.
For while drama clearly lies within what Susanne K. Langer calls "the
mode of Destiny"—springing along its vectors of project and action,
"always great with things to come"—it is no less characterized by
those moments when forward movement halts, when the dramatic
character must confront himself in the stillness and silence which
uniquely characterize the theater as an artistic medium. Typically, such
pauses are also moments of truth: the guiding motivation of a misperception collapses in the face of the real state of affairs, and the character
must reconstruct his understanding of himself and others in light of his
new realizations. Othello, driven by an increasingly blinding delusion,
is brought to the point where delusion ends, in the realization of how
he has been manipulated, what he has done, and how deeply it has

---

From *Modern Drama* 28, no. 4 (December 1985). © 1985 by the University of
Toronto, Graduate Centre for the Study of Drama.

cost him. Othello realizes—more fully and tragically—what he is, and his concluding speech reflects this insight: "I pray you, in your letters, / When you shall these unlucky deeds relate, / Speak of me as I am."

Although our Aristotelian heritage has stressed the centrality of such reversals and recognitions in tragic drama, it is arguable that comedy constitutes the more fertile ground for disillusionment as a dramatic subject. Comedy, after all, combines a conception of character organized much more tightly around fixed ideas with a principle of multiplication that generates increasingly intricate lines of action and brings characters into increasingly inevitable collision. Perhaps the most highly developed form of both these tendencies can be found in the comedies of Ben Jonson, where radically delineated characters—each dominated by a ruling preoccupation, or "humor"—are propelled along lines of action continually subject to interruption. Voltore, Corvino, and Corbaccio all hover around Volpone's sickbed, each driven by a notion of his own centrality deftly manipulated by the subtle Mosca. The logic of Jonsonian comedy leads to the exposure of these preoccupations, and individual characters suffer the sudden disillusionment of discovering that events are sharply different from what they supposed. Quintessentially Jonsonian, and typically comic, is the moment in act 5 of *Volpone* when the three suitors (and, to a lesser extent, Volpone and Mosca) stand gape-mouthed, "out of their humors," exposed to the Venetian Avocatori and to themselves.

No dramatist came closer to Jonson's fascination with delusion and disillusionment than George Bernard Shaw, whose plays are dramatic matrices of characters and their positions, animated by pulses of revelation. In this design, Shaw was helped (as he so often was) by his nineteenth-century dramatic backgrounds, particularly the legacy of the well-made play. This legacy provided Shaw with a dramaturgy founded on discrepant and incomplete awareness among characters, and a dramatic logic founded on misperception and subsequent discovery. A Scribean comedy sends a number of characters into motion, each lacking some important piece of the scheme of events, and multiplies the intricacy of error until it is resolved in a clarifying denouement. Disillusionment, the exposure of inaccurate understanding, is a sine qua non of the well-made play.

If "disillusionment" seems too strong a word for the moments of exposure in Scribean drama, it is because the consequences of illusions, and their loss, are in the end very slight. Error, in the world of the well-made play, constitutes an aberration, and its correction makes possible reconciliation and romance. In the denouement of Scribe's intrigue comedy *The Glass of Water,* for example, Queen Anne discovers that her ensign Masham, with whom she has been in love, is himself in love with a shopgirl; nevertheless, confronted with this jolting realization, she blesses their betrothal and turns her ever-roving eye on the handsome guardsman outside. Such characters may be temporarily ruled by *idées fixes,* but their illusions are flimsy things that may be abandoned or modified for the sake of the well-made-play resolution.

For the Shavian character, on the other hand, illusion and error occupy the realm of the self where he is most real and uncompromising: the realm of conviction. Shaw described his characters as "human being[s] possessed by . . . idea[s]," and their ideas accordingly serve as the structures through which they organize and express their vital energies. Even determinedly anti-ideological characters like Lady Britomart are possessed by ideas: not abstract notions, but complex and specific wholes, including codes of relationship, ethical distinctions, and private fictions that fuse conceptions of past and future to a notion of personal role often akin to a "calling." These complexes, the bulwarks of self-perception in Shaw's dramatic world, are more fiercely held even than the "life-lies" of *The Wild Duck* or the "pipe-dreams" of *The Iceman Cometh.*

Such personal constructs provide autonomy from certain aspects of life while facilitating participation in others, and their rupture implicates Shaw's characters with devastating suddenness in moral systems and networks of events and relationships against which they had previously found their moral identity. This crisis is generally precipitated by Scribean revelations of neglected fact which expose illusion by unearthing deeper levels of the truth. The central character of *Major Barbara,* for instance, begins her play with an evangelical divine scheme, a teleological vision cast against the complacency of the upper classes and the brutality of the lower: "Theyre all just the same sort of sinner: and theres the same salvation ready for them all." This conviction collapses into disillusionment when Barbara discovers that her salvation scheme, tragically conventional at the heart of its unconventionality, is incomplete, for it neglects the economic structure of society, the mechanisms of which derive the Salvation Army's financial backing from Bodger and Undershaft—sources who also fuel the social conditions which the Army seeks to redress. It neglects, too, human intransigence in this society: when Barbara learns that Snobby Price, newly repentant, has pocketed the coins left on the drum, she finds salvation at the service of greed. As so often in Shavian drama, reality ruptures the idealism which mistakes it, and Barbara must share Vivie Warren's earlier recognition when she learns in act 3 of *Mrs Warren's Profession* that her income has derived from the same system of exploitation that employs her mother: "I believe I am just as bad as you." Her convictions shattered, Barbara watches the Salvation Army march away in a parody of her missionary zeal.

For this kind of moral capitulation, "disillusionment" is probably too tame a word: recognition like this shares the nihilistic tones of Jonsonian exposure. Vivie's confession—"I feel among the damned already"—is no rhetorical trope; it reveals the depth of her sudden despair. Trench, in *Widowers' Houses* displays an almost Sartrean vertigo when confronted with the tainted sources of his money. Shaw's stage direction is explicit: "TRENCH *does not at once reply. He stares at* SARTORIUS, *and then hangs his head and gazes stupidly at the floor, morally beggared, with his clasped knuckles between his knees, a living picture of disillusion.*" Barbara's disillusionment is only slightly less visceral:

> I stood on the rock I thought eternal; and without a word of warning it reeled and crumbled under me. I was safe with an infinite wisdom watching me, an army marching to Salvation with me; and in a moment, at a stroke of your pen in a cheque book. I stood alone; and the heavens were empty. That was the first shock of the earthquake: I am waiting for the second.

If the dramatic technique of Scribe and the other well-made-play dramatists focused on the clarifications and resolutions of the truth learned, Shaw often chose to dwell on the "frightful irony" of illusions lost.

Shaw's interest in disillusionment and its consequences has a further dimension, one which ties his "drama of ideas" even more closely to the stage for which he wrote. When Shaw defined comedy as "the fine art of disillusion," he meant that comedy's function was to disrupt complacency and illusion as they existed both in the world of his characters and in the auditorium of the spectator. Ibsen's greatness,

Shaw maintained, lay primarily in his dramatic assault on his audience, his "terrible art of sharp-shooting at the audience, trapping them, fencing with them, aiming always at the sorest spot in their consciences." Beyond Ibsen's broader attack on the prejudices and outworn ideas of society at large, Shaw specifically praised his plot technique, the management of sequential action by which Ibsen attacked audience perception within the theater. "[T]he new school," Shaw wrote, "will trick the spectator into forming a meanly false judgment, and then convict him of it in the next act, often to his grievous mortification." To understand the precise way in which Shaw meant this kind of praise, and to lay some basis for our exploration of how Shaw put these principles to work in his own "sharp-shooting" drama, it is useful to sketch some observations concerning the ways in which the theater engages and shapes audience comprehension of what they see unfolding on stage. The theater audience, it will be suggested, like the dramatic character, are subjected to a unique tension between comprehension and its undermining.

To begin, one must recognize that the theater audience—unlike the reader of novels or other strictly textual narrative forms—construct their understanding of fictional events out of forms, movements, and sounds existing in the present, unmediated by an authorial consciousness through which they might be given significance and coherence. As Thornton Wilder points out:

A play is what takes place.

A novel is what one person tells us took place.

The theatrical insights of theorists like J. L. Styan and Bernard Beckerman notwithstanding, dramatic criticism has still not successfully explored the implications of this difference for dramatic concepts like "plot," "theme," and "character," and most discussions of drama persist in treating plays as slightly less sophisticated versions of textual literary forms (this approach is especially tempting with Shaw, whose literary presence in the printed versions of his plays is, of course, overwhelming). In discussions of dramatic narrative, or "plot," the tendency to ignore the performance features of a dramatic work reveals itself in a reliance on plot summary—the outline of events, conceived in retrospect—as the sole experience of a play's temporal outline. When the medium of performance is taken into account at all, it is tamed, with the audience cast as omniscient overseers in command of the play and all its outlines. Such a view of the audience-stage relationship underlies the traditional concept of "dramatic irony," as William Archer makes clear:

> We are, in fact, in the position of superior intelligences contemplating, with miraculous clairvoyance, the stumblings and fumblings of poor blind mortals straying through the labyrinth of life. Our seat in the theatre is like a throne on the Epicurean Olympus, whence we can view with perfect intelligence, but without participation or responsibility, the intricate reactions of human destiny.

But the final outline of events plays only a minor role in the audience's theatrical experience, and omniscience is far from complete. From the first moment of performance, audience comprehension and judgment consist of a complex process—probing to endow the materials and persons of the stage with fictional significance, projecting a tentative "past" and "future" out of given clues, seeking (when appropriate) to locate the characters and actions in familiar ethical categories, continually modifying this perceptual/conceptual structure in response to the confirmations and deflections of performance—which moves forward at a pace over which the spectator has no control. Comprehension of events in the theater is always provisional and—until the end of performance—necessarily incomplete. In its temporal unfolding, dramatic plot is a string of inferences, the moment's best guess.

Such an understanding of theatrical comprehension suggests that the audience's position in respect to the ongoing dramatic representation is significantly less than "Olympian." This has two important implications for drama in general, and for the Shavian "play of ideas" in particular. For one thing, the relative autonomy of theatrical performance from a ruling authorial point of view forces the dramatist to establish signals for temporal comprehension and ethical judgment within the dramatic world itself. Over the centuries, the dramatic repertoire has accumulated a wealth of devices and techniques to this end: juxtaposition of dramatic segments, use of known stories, "extradramatic" figures (prologue and epilogue characters, onstage commentators), *raisonneurs,* dramatic symbols, as well as other dramatic conventions. The Shavian canon displays Shaw's reliance on such devices and techniques. *Caesar and Cleopatra, The Man of Destiny,* and *Androcles and the Lion* join numerous other Shaw plays in proposing familiar historical events and characters as signifying contexts for onstage action. *Saint Joan* reveals a careful manipulation of setting and scene division to cast the worlds of court, camp, and countryside in ideological counterpoint. Moreover, few Shaw plays lack the central intellectual presence of the Shavian *raisonneur,* who orders and articulates the ranging social, economic, and ethical points of view, and who seems to hold the firmest grasp on events. True, each of these devices provides the opportunity for subverting audience expectations, but they do so while building patterns of coherence and comprehensibility against which subversion can operate. It is through such devices, one might say, that we see Shaw the dogmatist, working to impose order on the flux of performance just as, in his prose, he sought to impose order on history, behavior, and thought.

In many ways, *Major Barbara* constitutes the culmination of this impulse of Shavian dramaturgy, for Shaw constructed the play with a wealth of controls to streamline the temporal development and the thematic level which this development underscores. Shaw's three acts, for instance, break the setting into three locations and time spans stylized with an emblematic force reminiscent of morality drama or, to choose a literary text which Shaw greatly admired, of *Pilgrim's Progress:*

> UNDERSHAFT: . . . Where is your shelter?
> BARBARA: In West Ham. At the sign of the cross. Ask anybody in Canning Town. Where are your works?
> UNDERSHAFT: In Perivale St Andrews. At the sign of the sword. Ask anybody in Europe.

As the play unfolds, the contending ethical standpoints which these settings represent are displayed to the audience with almost Brechtian directness. Dramatic explicitness is especially pronounced in the second act, which Shaw called "a play in itself," and which features discrepant points of view set in overtly ironic relationship to each other: salvationism, Undershaftianism, and the violence and chicanery of West Ham itself. Character interactions highlight the contrasts: Jenny Hill with Snobby Price, Barbara with Bill Walker, Barbara with Undershaft, Undershaft with Mrs. Baines. The theatrical effect of such explicitness and contrast is an intense clarification of events and issues which reaches its ironic climax at the act's conclusion in the almost pictorial arrangement of points of view: Mrs. Baines receiving Undershaft's signed check ("The longer I live the more proof I see that there is an Infinite Goodness that turns everything to the work of salvation sooner or later"), Bill Walker looking on triumphantly, Barbara standing alone in her despair, and Cusins ecstatically drawing out the ironies:

"The millennium will be inaugurated by the unselfishness of Undershaft and Bodger. Oh be joyful!" Seldom is Shaw's ironic counterpoint—between discrepant understandings of events, and between these understandings and the stage action itself—so explicit.

Guided by this mutually illuminating opposition of points of view, by the clear demarcation of setting and action, and directed into the final act by the central soul-struggle between Barbara and Undershaft, the audience of *Major Barbara* are permitted a high degree of comprehension concerning the temporal and ideological development of what they see on the stage. In light of these features, one might be tempted to agree with Francis Fergusson that *Major Barbara* is a "thesis," shaped by its broad conceptual development—from Wilton Crescent to West Ham to Perivale St. Andrews—and by Barbara's conversion to reality within this scheme. As the play moves into its final act, though, it becomes clear that this development is undermined in significant ways, and that the theater audience find their Olympian comprehension of events and positions uncomfortably disturbed.

It is through such underminings and qualifications that we encounter the other Shaw, the theater artist who reveled in performance and all its potential anarchies. For, as the above remarks on audience response imply, theatrical performance exerts continual pressure against the structures of audience comprehension upon which temporal order and judgment rest. It does so, in part, through the inescapable relativity of the stage—the fact that every position and point of view must share the stage with other positions and points of view, each of which exerts its own claims to legitimacy. Lacking an authorial presence, in short, performance works to undermine the exclusivity of "authoritative" standpoints. The Devil's voice stubbornly refuses to be silenced during his debate with Don Juan, and Joan's visionary heroism must contend with the Dauphin's worldly timidity. Indeed, confrontation frequently edges into deflation, as it does when Cleopatra informs Caesar that the object of his lyrical tribute "isnt the great Sphinx," or when Ann Whitefield closes *Man and Superman* by telling Tanner to "Go on talking." More fundamentally, performance tends to undermine all structures of comprehension which the audience build, through its unmediated presence and the fact of its temporal unfolding. Since performance is always slightly beyond comprehension's reach, continually edging into the unknown, it repeatedly pressures comprehension with unintelligibility and even, at times, with collapse. An unexpected revelation, a moment of complicated stage action, the undermining of a controlling device—and a spectator's understanding of temporal and ethical relationships lapses into momentary bewilderment; comprehension, with all its intricacies, reverts to a less ordered apprehension of the dramatic present and its immediacy.

Performance, then, subjects the audience to rhythms of comprehension and its undermining significantly analogous to movements of understanding and "disillusionment" within the dramatic world. Audience comprehension is never held with the conviction of character illusion, nor is its surrender as devastating, for the aesthetic nature of dramatic representation guarantees that our construction of a play's temporal meanings never has the personal consequence with which we invest our private roles, fictions, and judgments. But to the extent to which our comprehension of dramatic events and their significance does constitute the generation and structuring of meaning, then its undermining is a kind of "disillusionment," one which returns us— like Othello, Voltore, and Barbara—to a world which lies outside our structures of meaning, even if this world is the safe one of the stage. It is this return to the immediacy of performance, as well as the dramatic character's self-confrontation in stillness, which constitutes the theater's most important gift to drama: the gift of presence.

Manipulation of this kind of audience disillusionment represents a powerful element of dramatic art, one frequently neglected in dramatic criticism as a result of dramatic theory's exclusive focus on comprehension and coherence as aesthetic values. Jonsonian comedy, for instance, continually stretches comprehension along routes of escalating intricacy, deliberately causing structures of coherence and meaning to collapse against the multiplicity of incident—a dramaturgical reflection of Jonson's thematic concern with the boundaries of the self and its cognitive constructs. Indeed, even the well-made play draws upon this kind of theatrical manipulation. Ideally, the well-made play hinges on a secret which, although withheld from a character, is known or suspected by the audience. In practice, though, the secret is often hidden from the audience as well, or withheld to the extent that its disclosure forces a significant restructuring of audience comprehension. In act 2 of *The Glass of Water,* for instance, the revelation of Queen Anne's love for Masham, while it has been hinted at, nevertheless forces the audience to review their memory of events and revise their understanding of character relationships and the dilemmas they involve. Still, the bias of the well-made play remains toward comprehension, for its dramatists conceived of the audience in a position of ironic superiority over events—as participants in the theatrical interaction whose faculties might be teased, but whose cognitive and ethical constructions would, in the end, be upheld. Reflecting this bias, Archer and other turn-of-the-century drama theorists argued for the dramatic value of "suspense" and "curiosity," but insisted upon the boundaries beyond which toying with comprehension was unwise.

Shaw, antagonistic to such boundaries as he was to all limits of his audience's faculties, pushed surprise into shock on many occasions and frequently manipulated his audience's comprehension of events as ruthlessly as he did his characters'. The remarks of Cleopatra and Ann come as shocks to the audience as well as to Caesar and Tanner: they force sudden disruptions in response, pressing understanding back into bewilderment, if ever so briefly. Similarly, the report of Ferrovius blindly slaying the Roman gladiators in the final act of *Androcles and the Lion,* unprepared for, drops the audience's expectation momentarily into chaos. The instances of such effects are legion in Shaw, and we must not use our retrospective familiarity with outcomes to downplay their theatrical impact.

In even so streamlined a play as *Major Barbara,* disruption emerges to shake the audience with its force and confusion. After a brief respite in Wilton Crescent at the start of act 3, the scene shifts to Undershaft's domain. Up until this point, Undershaft has served as *raisonneur,* guiding audience perspective through his irrefutable insight into the events and ethical stances of the play's world: "You shall see. All religious organizations exist by selling themselves to the rich." With its almost "divine right" historical succession, his ideology becomes the seemingly inevitable replacement for Barbara's shattered salvationism. When Undershaft's world becomes the dramatic setting, however, his position becomes disturbingly problematic for an audience who have been led to accept it. Earlier in the play, Undershaft's critical authority was displayed in situations where he stood outside, or to one side, of events, calling attention to the truth beneath worlds other than his own. The gunpowder shed, on the other hand, so potentially explosive that single matches must be dropped into a fire bucket, reveals that Undershaft's prophetic insight does not necessarily imply control. Paradoxically, the massive power of the foundry serves to expose Undershaft's personal powerlessness, and he admits this: "It does not belong to me. I belong to it." As he later warns Cusins: "From the moment when you become Andrew Undershaft, you will never do as you please again. Dont come here lusting for power, young man."

This powerlessness has distinct dramatic implications for the play's conclusion and how it is experienced in the theater. Where we might expect events to shape themselves toward a resolution, onstage or projected, the future fades into uncertainty, for Undershaft's moral vision is now shown to lack an end that might guide the incredible power which he has amassed. When asked by Cusins: "And what drives the place?" he replies "(*enigmatically*) A will of which I am a part." However, in the range of voices occupying the stage in this final act, such a statement cannot escape the darker echoes of Cusins's initial response to the foundry and its city in this distance: "Not a ray of hope." Undershaft offers his armaments to all buyers, and Cusins's accusation that the foundry is actually "driven by the most rascally part of society, the money hunters, the pleasure hunters, the military promotion hunters; and he is their slave" is never satisfactorily answered. The overwhelming theatrical impact of the physical setting, its cannon trained on the background, reflects the dangerous amorality of Undershaft's philosophy and the threat implicit in its open-endedness. As Robert F. Whitman points out: "The failing of Undershaft's religion . . . is that all his money and gunpowder have no purpose, no goal, except to create themselves and perpetuate themselves. And it carries in itself the seeds of its own destruction." With a dramatic twist midway between Ibsen and Pirandello, Shaw renders problematic the play's apparent ethical center: the realist credo against which vision has already crumbled.

True, Barbara reasserts the claims of salvation in the play's closing moments, proclaiming a new mission through the synthesis of evangelical vision with Undershaftian realism: "through the raising of hell to heaven and of man to God, through the unveiling of an eternal light in the Valley of The Shadow." Ostensibly, vision has restored its teleological harness on the power of the present. But the synthesis of Shaw's dialectical marriage remains problematic for an audience who have witnessed the collapse of salvationism and, by implication, of all ideologies that seek to project beyond the present. Shaw provides no evidence that illusion has not been replaced by further illusion, no suggestion of how any visionary scheme will survive the earthquake's second shock when it arrives. As Barbara stands on the battlements, dummies sprawled in straw at her feet, the future remains ominously obscure. By this point, disillusionment has crossed the boundary between play and audience: in one of the culminating ironies of *Major Barbara,* Barbara's "return to the colors" takes place opposite deepening audience apprehension.

But the play's final-act disillusionment is also a liberation, and a theatrical one at that. For as the conceptual clarity of the previous acts gives way to uncertainty and ambivalence, the stage itself stands out with increasing autonomy, free of subjugating theses and narrative lines. Cluttered with props and actors, pervaded by an atmosphere of awe, the stage becomes a space of energy in itself, a contagious space which the audience cannot help but share. In this regard, the conclusion constitutes an appropriate climax for the play as a whole. Shaw may have claimed that *Major Barbara* was about poverty, but it deals much more fundamentally—as does all of Shavian drama—with power, in all of its forms: Blood and Fire, Money and Gunpowder. Power courses through the play's confrontations: Lady Britomart with Stephen, Barbara with Bill Walker, and Undershaft with Barbara, as he looks hypnotically in her eyes and asks: "Tell him, my love, what power really means." Drums roll, horns play, people march in ecstatic procession, a stage setting looms huge with explosive power. Such power is death, but it is also life, and in both capacities it lies in uneasy relationship to personal frameworks that seek to control or deny it. In moments when these frameworks weaken, it exists in unmediated presence, both for the characters who grapple with it and for the theater audience who witness its triumph.

Both dogmatist and theater artist, then, Shaw combined a commitment to the coherence of events and ideas with a persistent disillusioning impulse designed to undercut the structures of comprehension which support this coherence. In the confrontation of these two impulses, alternately deliberate and ambivalent, we can recognize the source of both the power and the difficulty of Shavian drama, since a Shaw play derives its characteristic rhythms less from the clear comprehension of certain "ideas" than from the energy with which it confronts comprehension itself. Writing anonymously about *Major Barbara* in 1915, Shaw made a pertinent remark: "It made demands on the audience but the demands were conceded. The audience left the theater exhausted, but felt the better for it and came again."

Chronology

1856	Born on July 26, in Dublin, Ireland.
1876	Moves to London in hopes of professional advancement and becomes a small-time journalist.
1879	Hired by the Edison Telephone Company and completes his first novel, *Immaturity*.
1880	Writes a second novel, *The Irrational Knot*. Joins the Dialectical Society.
1881	Becomes a vegetarian in an attempt to cure migraine headaches and takes lessons in boxing. Writes *Love among the Artists*.
1882	Converts to socialism and completes his best novel, *Cashel Byron's Profession*.
1884	Falls among the Fabians. *An Unsocial Socialist* is serialized.
1885	Father dies.
1886–88	Works as an art critic and music critic for various journals.
1889	Publishes *Fabian Essays*.
1890	Begins work as a music critic for *The World*. Lectures to the Fabian Society on Ibsen.
1891	Publishes *The Quintessence of Ibsenism*.
1892–93	*Widowers' Houses*, *The Philanderer*, *Mrs Warren's Profession*.
1894	*Arms and the Man*, *Candida*.
1895	Starts as drama critic for the *Saturday Review*. *The Man of Destiny*, *You Never Can Tell*.
1896	*The Devil's Disciple*.
1898	Marries Charlotte Payne-Townshend. *Caesar and Cleopatra*, *The Perfect Wagnerite*.
1899	*Captain Brassbound's Conversion*.
1903	*Man and Superman*.
1904	*John Bull's Other Island*.

1905	Visits Ireland. *Major Barbara*.
1906	Meets Ellen Terry. *The Doctor's Dilemma, Our Theatre in the Nineties*.
1908	*Getting Married*.
1909	*Misalliance, The Shewing-up of Blanco Posnet*.
1911	*Fanny's First Play*.
1912	*Androcles and the Lion, Pygmalion*. Friendship with Mrs. Patrick Campbell.
1914	*Common Sense about the War*.
1916–19	*Heartbreak House*.
1920	*Back to Methuselah*.
1923	*Saint Joan*.
1926	Receives the Nobel Prize for literature—uses the prize money to support the publication of translations from Swedish literature.
1928	*The Intelligent Woman's Guide to Socialism, Capitalism, Sovietism, and Fascism*.
1929	*The Apple Cart*.
1931	*Ellen Terry and Bernard Shaw: A Correspondence*. Travels to U.S.S.R.
1932	*The Adventures of the Black Girl in Her Search for God*.
1933	Goes to America.
1934	*Collected Prefaces*.
1939	*In Good King Charles's Golden Days*.
1943	Wife dies.
1944	*Everybody's Political What's What*.
1950	Dies on November 13.

Contributors

HAROLD BLOOM, Sterling Professor of the Humanities at Yale University, is the author of *The Anxiety of Influence, Poetry and Repression,* and many other volumes of literary criticism. His forthcoming study, *Freud: Transference and Authority,* attempts a full-scale reading of all of Freud's major writings. A MacArthur Prize Fellow, he is general editor of five series of literary criticism published by Chelsea House. During 1987–88, he served as Charles Eliot Norton Professor of Poetry at Harvard University.

BARBARA BELLOW WATSON teaches English at the City College of New York. She is author of *The Shavian Guide to the Intelligent Woman.* Her poetry as well as her criticism appears in *The New Yorker, Prairie Schooner, Kenyon Review,* and *Harper's.*

WILLIAM G. MCCOLLOM was Professor of English and Dramatic Arts at Case Western Reserve University. He wrote *Tragedy* and *The Divine Average: A View of Comedy,* as well as many articles.

MARGERY M. MORGAN is Reader in English at the University of Lancaster. She is author of *A Drama of Political Man: A Study in the Plays of Harley Granville-Barker* and *The Shavian Playground.*

J. L. WISENTHAL is Professor of English at the University of British Columbia and editor of *Shaw and Ibsen: Bernard Shaw's* The Quintessence of Ibsenism *and Related Writings.*

ALFRED TURCO, JR., teaches English at Wesleyan University.

J. PERCY SMITH, formerly Vice President of the University of Guelph, Canada, is Professor Emeritus of Drama. He has published extensively on Shaw.

STANTON B. GARNER, JR., is Professor of Drama at the University of Michigan.

Bibliography

Adams, Elsie B. *Bernard Shaw and the Aesthetes.* Columbus: Ohio State University Press, 1972.

——. "Feminism and Female Stereotypes in Shaw." *Shaw Review* 17 (1974): 17–22.

Albert, Sidney P. "More Shaw Advice to the Players of Major Barbara." *Theatre Studies* 11 (1970): 66–85.

——. "Reflections on Shaw and Psychoanalysis." *Modern Drama* 3 (1971): 169–94.

——. "The Price of Salvation: Moral Economics in *Major Barbara*." *Modern Drama* 14 (1971): 307–23.

Appasamy, S. P. "God, Mammon, and Bernard Shaw." *Commonwealth Quarterly* 2, no. 7 (1978): 98–112.

Baker, Stuart E. "Logic and Religion in *Major Barbara*: The Syllogism of St. Andrew Undershaft." *Modern Drama* 21 (1978): 241–52.

Barr, Alan P. *Victorian Stage Pulpiteer: Bernard Shaw's Crusade.* Athens: University of Georgia Press, 1973.

Baskin, Ken A. "Undershaft's Challenge and the Future of the Race." *Shaw Review* 21 (1978): 136–51.

Bentley, Eric. "Ibsen, Shaw, Brecht: Three Stages." In *The Rarer Action: Essays in Honor of Francis Fergusson,* edited by Alan Chese and Richard Koffler, 3–24. New Brunswick: Rutgers University Press, 1970.

——. *The Playwright as Thinker.* New York: Reynal & Hitchcock, 1946.

Berst, Charles A. *Bernard Shaw and the Art of Drama.* Urbana: University of Illinois Press, 1973.

——, ed. *Shaw and Religion.* University Park: Pennsylvania State University Press, 1981.

Caudwell, Christopher. "George Bernard Shaw: A Study of the Bourgeois Superman." In *Five Approaches of Literary Criticism,* edited by Wilbur S. Scott. New York: Collier, 1962.

Chesterton, G. K. *George Bernard Shaw.* New York: Folcroft Library Editions, 1978.

Coskren, Robert. "Wagner and Shaw: *Rheingold* Motifs in *Major Barbara*." *Comparative Drama* 14 (1980): 70–73.

Crane, Gladys M. "Shaw and Women's Lib." *Shaw Review* 17 (1974): 23–31.

Crompton, Louis. *Shaw the Dramatist.* Lincoln: University of Nebraska Press, 1969.

Dukore, Bernard F. *Bernard Shaw, Director*. Seattle: University of Washington Press, 1971.

———. *Bernard Shaw, Playwright: Aspects of Shavian Drama*. Columbia: University of Missouri Press, 1973.

———. "Revising *Major Barbara*." *Shaw Review* 16 (1973): 2–10.

———. "The Time of *Major Barbara*." *Theatre Studies* 23 (1982): 110–11.

Ellman, Richard, ed. *Edwardians and Late Victorians: Essays of the English Institute*. New York: Columbia University Press, 1960.

Evans, T. F., ed. *Shaw: The Critical Heritage*. London: Routledge & Kegan Paul, 1976.

Fiske, Irving. *Bernard Shaw's Debt to William Blake*. London: The Shaw Society (Shavian Tract no. 2), 1951.

Forter, Elizabeth T., ed. *Major Barbara*. New York: Appleton-Century-Crofts, 1971.

Frank, Joseph. "*Major Barbara*—Shaw's Divine Comedy." *PMLA* 72 (1956): 61–74.

Frankel, Charles. "Efficient Power and Inefficient Virtue (Bernard Shaw: *Major Barbara*)." In *Great Moral Dilemmas in Literature, Past and Present*, edited by R. M. McIver. New York: New York Institute for Religious and Social Studies, 1956.

Furlong, William B. *GBS/GKC: Shaw and Chesterton, the Metaphysical Jesters*. University Park: Pennsylvania State University Press, 1970.

Gassner, John. *Ideas in the Drama*. New York: Columbia University Press, 1964.

Gelber, Norman. "The 'Misalliance' Theme in *Major Barbara*." *Shaw Review* 15 (1972): 65–70.

Gibbs, A. M. *The Art and Mind of Shaw*. London: Macmillan, 1983.

Gordon, David J. "Literature and Repression: The Case of Shavian Drama." In *The Literary Freud: Mechanisms of Defense and the Poetic Will*, edited by Joseph H. Smith, 181–203. New Haven: Yale University Press, 1980.

Grene, Nicholas. *Bernard Shaw: A Critical View*. London: Macmillan, 1984.

Harris, Frank. *Bernard Shaw*. Garden City, N.Y.: Garden City Publishing, 1931.

Harrison, D. B. "A New Source for Shaw's *Major Barbara*." *English Literature in Transition* 28 (1985): 56–58.

Holroyd, Michael, ed. *The Genius of Shaw: A Symposium*. New York: Holt, 1979.

Hugo, Leon. "*Major Barbara* at the Court." *UNISA English Studies* 9, no. 2 (1971): 1–6.

Hummert, Paul A. *Bernard Shaw's Marxian Romance*. Lincoln: University of Nebraska Press, 1973.

Irvine, William. *The Universe of G.B.S.* New York: Whittlesey House, 1949.

Jewkes, W. T. "The Faust Theme in *Major Barbara*." *Shaw Review* 21 (1978): 80–91.

Jordan, Robert J. "Theme and Character in *Major Barbara*." *Texas Studies in Literature and Language* 12 (1970): 471–80.

Kaufmann, R. J., ed. *G. B. Shaw: A Collection of Critical Essays*. Englewood Cliffs, N.J.: Prentice-Hall, 1965.

Kaul, A. N. *The Action of English Comedy: Studies in the Encounter of Abstraction and Experience from Shakespeare to Shaw*. New Haven: Yale University Press, 1970.

Kennedy, Andrew K. *Six Dramatists in Search of a Language: Studies in Dramatic Language*. London: Cambridge University Press, 1975.

Leary, Daniel J. "Dialectical Action in *Major Barbara*." *Shaw Review* 12 (1969): 46–58.

Lefcourt, Charles R. "Major Barbara: An Exercise in Shavian Wit and Wisdom." *English Review* 25, no. 2 (1974): 27–29.

Lorichs, Sonja. *The Unwomanly Woman in Bernard Shaw's Drama and Her Social and Political Background.* Uppsala, Sweden: Almqvist & Wiksell, 1973.

MacCarthy, Desmond. *Shaw.* London: MacGibbon & Kee, 1951.

Mander, Raymond, and Joe Mitchenson. *Theatrical Companion to Shaw: A Pictorial Record of the First Performances of the Plays of George Bernard Shaw.* New York: Pitman, 1955.

May, Keith M. *Ibsen and Shaw.* New York: St. Martin's, 1985.

Mayne, Fred. *The Wit and Satire of Bernard Shaw.* New York: St. Martin's, 1967.

McCollom, William G. *The Divine Average: A View of Comedy.* Cleveland: Press of Case Western Reserve University, 1971.

Meisel, Martin. *Shaw and the Nineteenth Century Theatre.* Princeton: Princeton University Press, 1969.

Mencken, H. L. *George Bernard Shaw: His Plays.* Boston: John W. Luce & Co., 1905.

Mills, John A. *Language and Laughter: Comic Diction in the Plays of Bernard Shaw.* Tucson: University of Arizona Press, 1969.

Mix, Katherine. "Max on Shaw." In *The Surprise of Excellence: Modern Essays on Max Beerbohm,* edited by J. G. Riewald, 131–37. Hamden, Conn.: Archon, 1974.

Morgan, Margery G. *The Shavian Playground: An Exploration of the Art of George Bernard Shaw.* London: Methuen, 1972.

Morsberger, Robert E. "The Winning of Barbara Undershaft: Conversion by the Cannon Factory, or 'Wot Prawce Selvytion nah?' " *Costerus* 9 (1973): 71–77.

Nelson, Raymond S. "Responses to Poverty in *Major Barbara*." *Arizona Quarterly* 27 (1971): 335–46.

Nethercot, Arthur H. *Men and Supermen: The Shavian Portrait Gallery.* 2d ed. Salem, N.H.: Ayer, 1966.

Newby, Richard L. "An Arnoldian Allusion in *Major Barbara*." *American Notes and Queries* 16 (1978): 68.

Nickson, Richard. "The Art of Shavian Political Drama." *Modern Drama* 14 (1971): 324–30.

Noel, Thomas. "Major Barbara and Her Male Generals." *Shaw Review* 22 (1979): 135–41.

Nutter, Norma. "Belief and Reality in *Major Barbara*." *Shaw Review* 22 (1979): 89–91.

O'Donovan, John, *G. B. Shaw.* Dublin: Gill & Macmillan, 1983.

Ohmann, Richard M. *Shaw: The Style and the Man.* Middletown, Conn.: Wesleyan University Press, 1962.

Pedersen, Lise. "Ducats and Daughter in *The Merchant of Venice* and *Major Barbara*." *Shaw Review* 4 (1984): 69–86.

Potter, Rosanne G. "The Rhetoric of a Shavian Exposition: Act 1 of *Major Barbara*." *Modern Drama* 26 (1983): 62–74.

Rosador, Kurt T. von. "The Natural History of *Major Barbara*." *Modern Drama* 17 (1974): 141–53.

Rosenblood, Norman, ed. *Shaw: Seven Critical Essays*. Toronto: University of Toronto Press, 1971.

Roy, R. N. *George Bernard Shaw's Historical Plays*. Delhi: Macmillan, 1976.

Russell, Annie. "George Bernard Shaw at Rehearsals of *Major Barbara*." *Shaw Review* 19 (1976): 73–82.

The Shaw Review 20 (1977). Special Shaw issue.

Silver, Arnold. *Bernard Shaw: The Darker Side*. Stanford: Stanford University Press, 1982.

Smith, J. Percy. *The Unrepentant Pilgrim*. Boston: Houghton Mifflin, 1965.

Smith, Warren S., ed. *Bernard Shaw's Plays*. New York: Norton, 1971.

Speckhard, Robert R. "Shaw and Aristophanes: Symbolic Marriage and the Magical Doctor/Cook in Shavian Comedy." *Shaw Review* 9 (1966): 56–65.

Turco, Alfred, Jr. *Shaw's Moral Vision: The Self and Salvation*. Ithaca: Cornell University Press, 1976.

Ure, Peter. "Master and Pupil in Bernard Shaw." *Essays in Criticism* 19, no.2 (April 1969): 118–39.

Valency, Maurice J. *The Cart and the Trumpet: The Plays of George Bernard Shaw*. New York: Oxford University Press, 1973.

Wall, Vincent. *Bernard Shaw: Pygmalion to Many Players*. Ann Arbor: University of Michigan Press, 1973.

Weintraub, Rodelle, ed. *Fabian Feminist*. University Park: Pennsylvania State University Press, 1977.

Weintraub, Stanley. "Bernard Shaw (review of research)." In *Anglo-Irish Literature: A Review of Research*, edited by Richard J. Finneran. New York: Modern Language Association, 1976.

———. "Exploiting Art: The Pictures in Bernard Shaw's Plays." *Modern Drama* 18 (1975): 215–38.

———. "Four Fathers for Major Barbara." In *Directions in Literary Criticism: Contemporary Approaches to Literature*, edited by Stanley Weintraub and Philip Young, 201–10. University Park: Pennsylvania State University Press, 1973.

———. *Journey to Heartbreak: The Crucible Years of Bernard Shaw, 1914–1918*. New York: Weybright & Talley, 1971.

———. *The Unexpected Shaw: Biographical Approaches to G.B.S. and His Work*. New York: Ungar, 1982.

West, Alick. *George Bernard Shaw: "A Good Man Fallen among Fabians."* New York: International Publishers, 1950.

Whitman, Robert F. *Shaw and the Play of Ideas*. Ithaca: Cornell University Press, 1977.

Whittock, Trevor. "*Major Barbara*: Comic Masterpiece." *Theoria* 51 (1978): 1–14.

Williams, Raymond. *Drama from Ibsen to Brecht*. New York: Oxford University Press, 1968.

Wilson, Colin. *Bernard Shaw: A Reassessment*. London: Hutchinson, 1969.

Wilson, Edmund. *The Triple Thinkers*. New York: Oxford University Press, 1963.

Wisenthal, J. L. *The Marriage of Contraries: Bernard Shaw's Middle Plays*. Cambridge: Harvard University Press, 1974.

———. "The Underside of Undershaft: A Wagnerian Motif in *Major Barbara*." *Shaw Review* 15 (1972): 56–64.

Woodbridge, Homer E. *George Bernard Shaw: Creative Artist*. Carbondale: Southern Illinois University Press, 1963.

Zimbardo, Rose, ed. *Twentieth Century Interpretations of* Major Barbara: *A Collection of Critical Essays*. Englewood Cliffs, N.J.: Prentice-Hall, 1970.

Acknowledgments

"Sainthood for Millionaires" (originally entitled "Sainthood for Millionaires: *Major Barbara*") by Barbara Bellow Watson from *Modern Drama* 11, no. 3 (December 1968), © 1968 by A. C. Edwards. Reprinted by permission.

"Shaw's Comedy and *Major Barbara*" by William G. McCollom from *The Divine Average: A View of Comedy* by William G. McCollom, © 1971 by the Press of Case Western Reserve University. Reprinted by permission of Case Western Reserve University, Cleveland, Ohio.

"Skeptical Faith" (originally entitled "*Major Barbara*") by Margery M. Morgan from *The Shavian Playground* by Margery M. Morgan, © 1972 by Margery M. Morgan. Reprinted by permission of Methuen & Co. Ltd.

"The Marriage of Contraries" (originally entitled "*Major Barbara*") by J. L. Wisenthal from *The Marriage of Contraries: Bernard Shaw's Middle Plays* by J. L. Wisenthal, © 1974 by the President and Fellows of Harvard College. Reprinted by permission of the publisher, Harvard University Press.

"Shaw's Moral Vision" (originally entitled "*Major Barbara*") by Alfred Turco, Jr., from *Shaw's Moral Vision: The Self and Salvation* by Alfred Turco, Jr., © 1976 by Cornell University. Reprinted by permission of the publisher, Cornell University Press. All quotations from Shaw's writings are used by permission of The Society of Authors and The Public Trustee.

"Shaw's Own Problem Play" by J. Percy Smith from *English Studies in Canada* 4, no. 4 (Winter 1978), © 1978 by the Association of Canadian University Teachers of English. Reprinted by permission of the Association.

"Shaw's Comedy of Disillusionment" by Stanton B. Garner, Jr., from *Modern Drama* 28, no. 4 (December 1985), © 1985 by the University of Toronto, Graduate Centre for the Study of Drama. Reprinted by permission.

Index